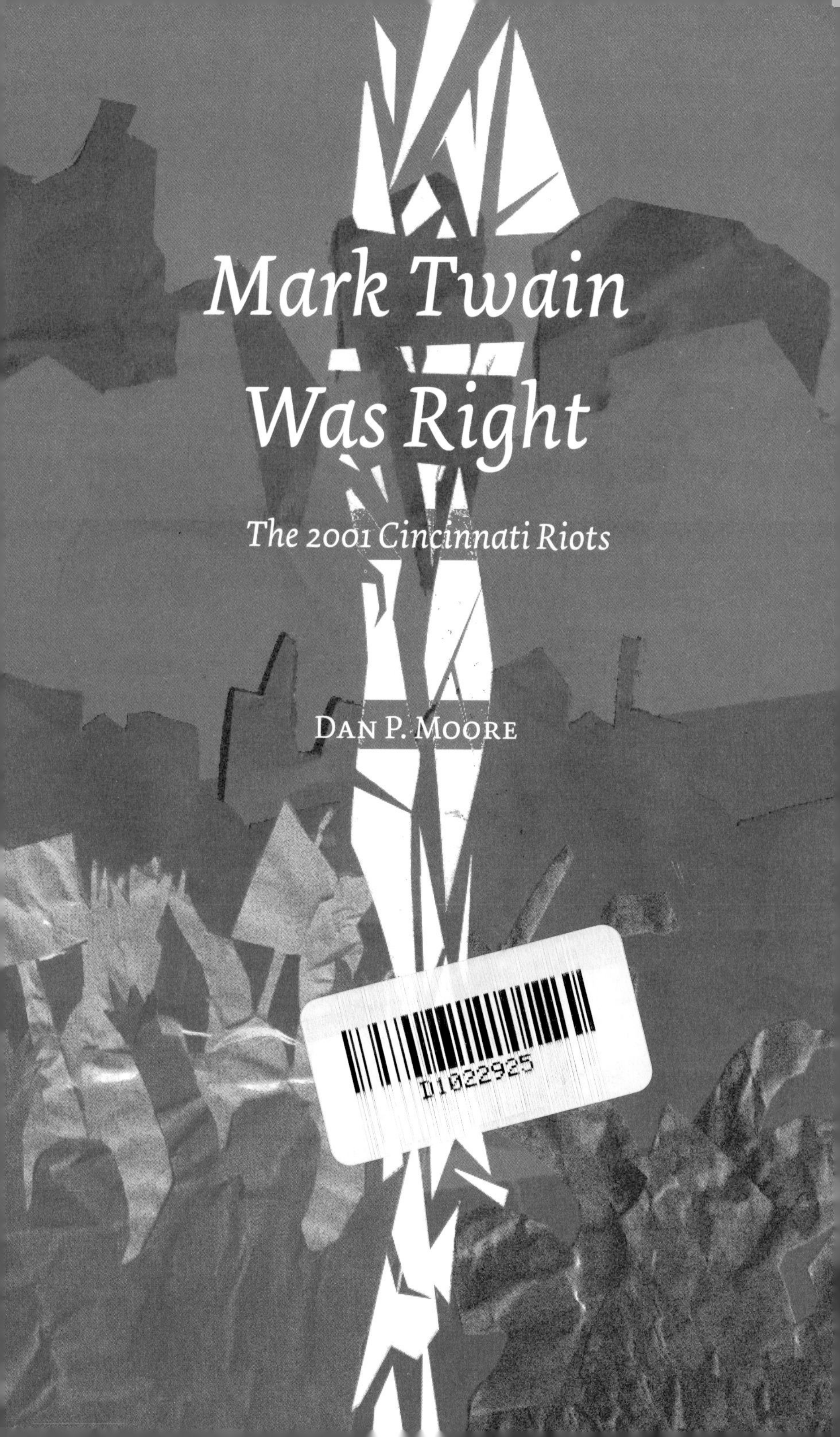

Mark Twain Was Right

The 2001 Cincinnati Riots

Dan P. Moore

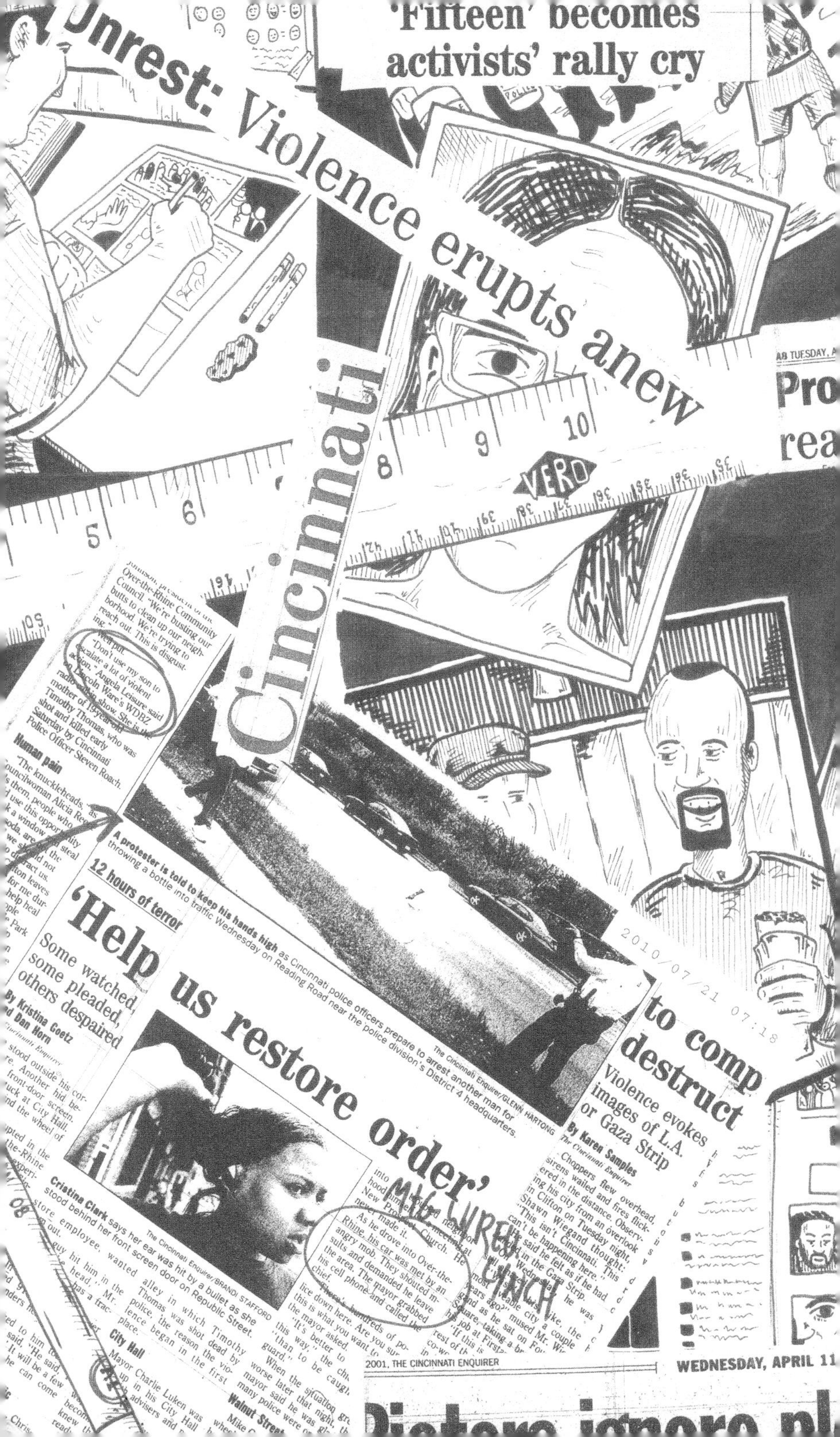
'Fifteen' becomes activists' rally cry
Unrest: Violence erupts anew
Cincinnati
A8 TUESDAY, A
Pro
rea
VERO
'Help us restore order'
12 hours of terror
Some watched, some pleaded, others despaired
to comp destruct
Violence evokes images of L.A. or Gaza Strip
By Karen Samples
A protester is told to keep his hands high as Cincinnati police officers prepare to arrest another man for throwing a bottle into traffic Wednesday on Reading Road near the police division's District 4 headquarters.
The Cincinnati Enquirer/GLENN HARTONG
Cristina Clark says her ear was hit by a bullet as she stood behind her front screen door on Republic Street.
The Cincinnati Enquirer/BRANDI STAFFORD
"Don't use my son to escalate a lot of violent action," Angela Leisure said on Lincoln Ware's WDBZ radio talk show. She is the mother of 19-year-old Timothy Thomas, who was shot and killed early Saturday by Cincinnati Police Officer Steven Roach.
Human pain
City Hall
2001, THE CINCINNATI ENQUIRER
WEDNESDAY, APRIL 11
2010/07/21 07:18

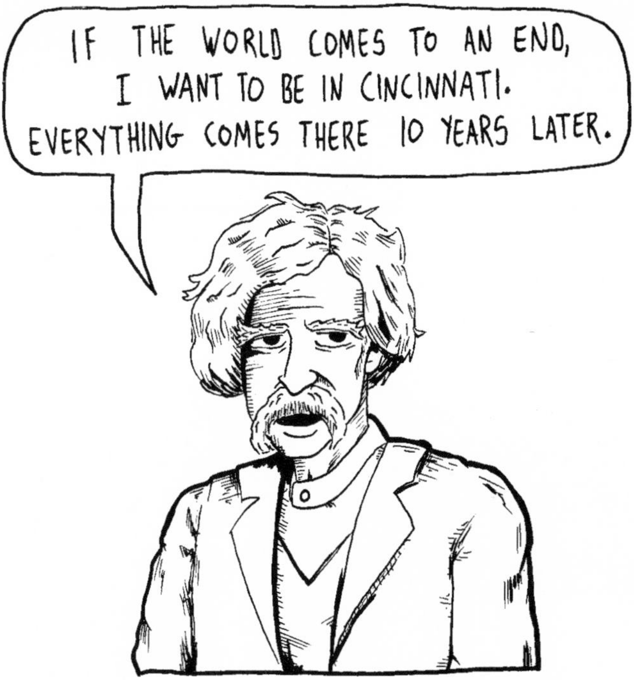
IF THE WORLD COMES TO AN END,
I WANT TO BE IN CINCINNATI.
EVERYTHING COMES THERE 10 YEARS LATER.

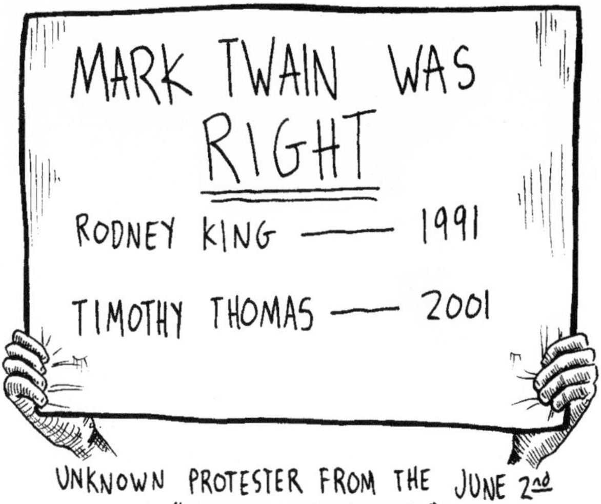
MARK TWAIN WAS
RIGHT
RODNEY KING —— 1991
TIMOTHY THOMAS —— 2001

UNKNOWN PROTESTER FROM THE JUNE 2nd 2001 "MARCH FOR JUSTICE"

MARK TWAIN WAS RIGHT
The 2001 Cincinnati Riots

by Dan P. Moore

Cover by Matt "The Option" Gauck
Edited by Joe Biel
Designed by Joe Biel

Published by:

Microcosm Publishing
112C S. Main St.
Lansing, KS 66043-1501
&
636 SE 11th Ave.
Portland, OR 97214
www.microcosmpublishing.com

ISBN 978-1-934620-21-2
This is Microcosm #76132

First Published October 1, 2012
First printing of 3,000 copies

Distributed by
Independent Publisher's Group, Chicago

Printed by
Thomson-Shore, Ann Arbor

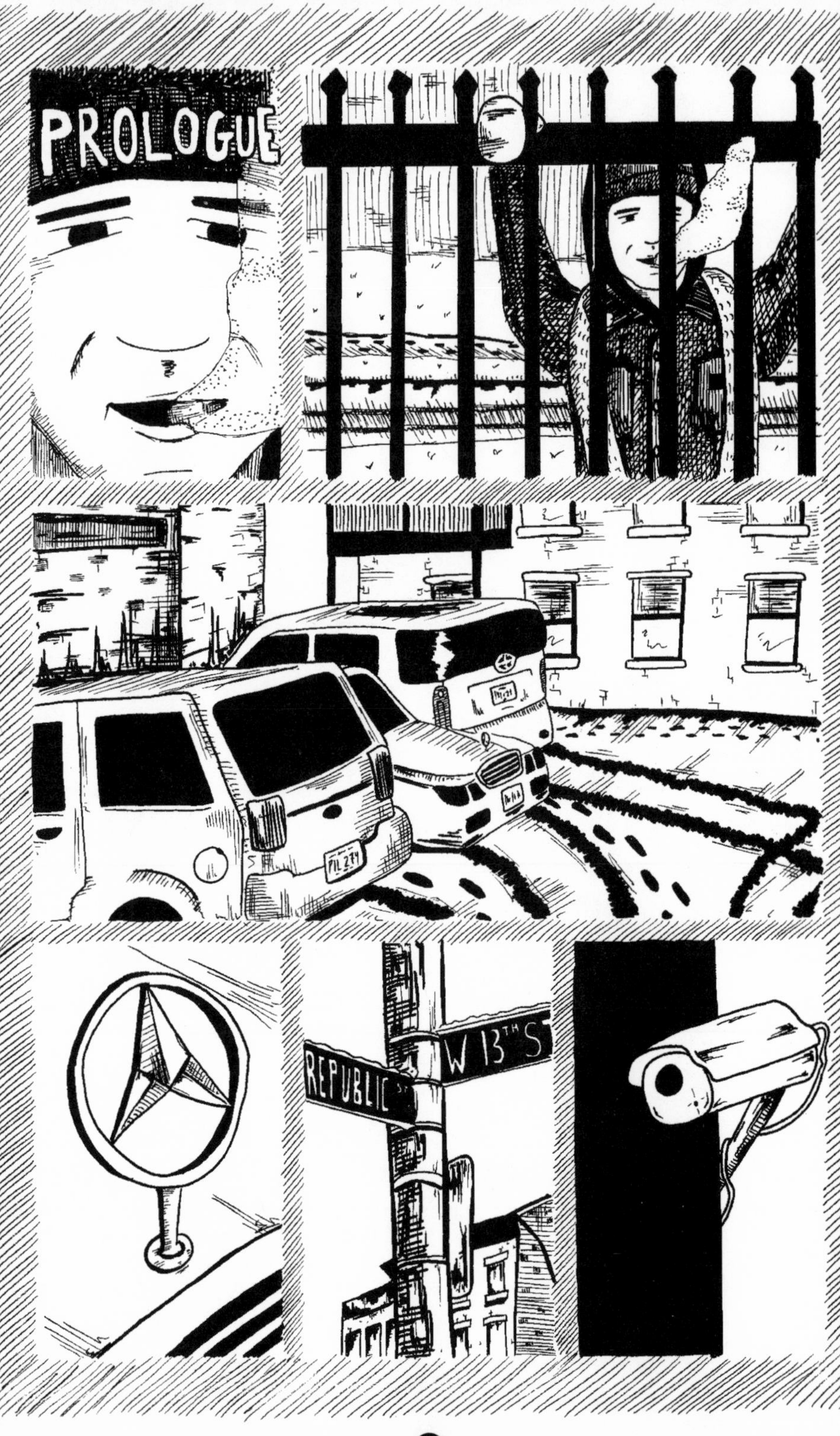
PROLOGUE
PIL 274
REPUBLIC ST
W 13TH S

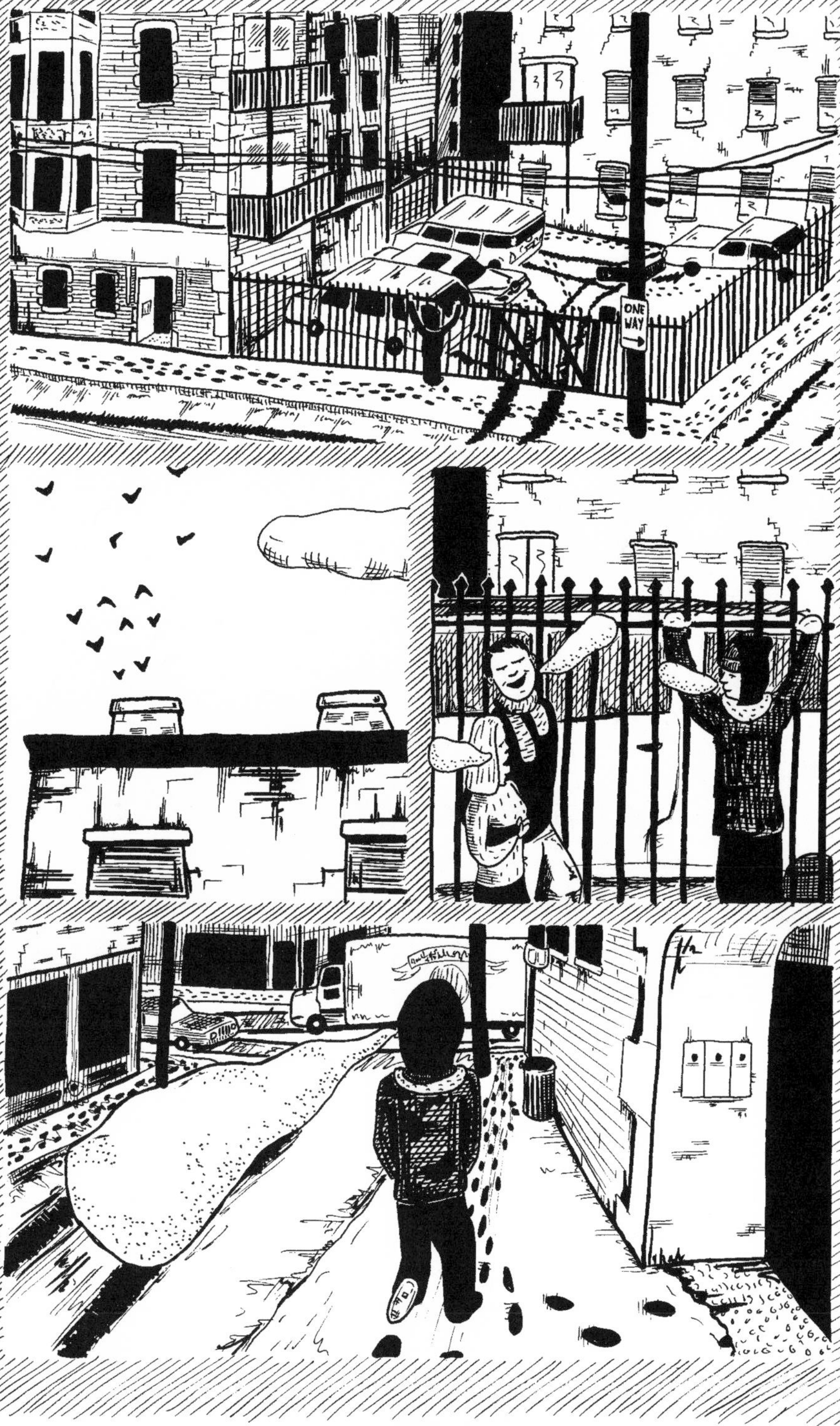
ONE WAY

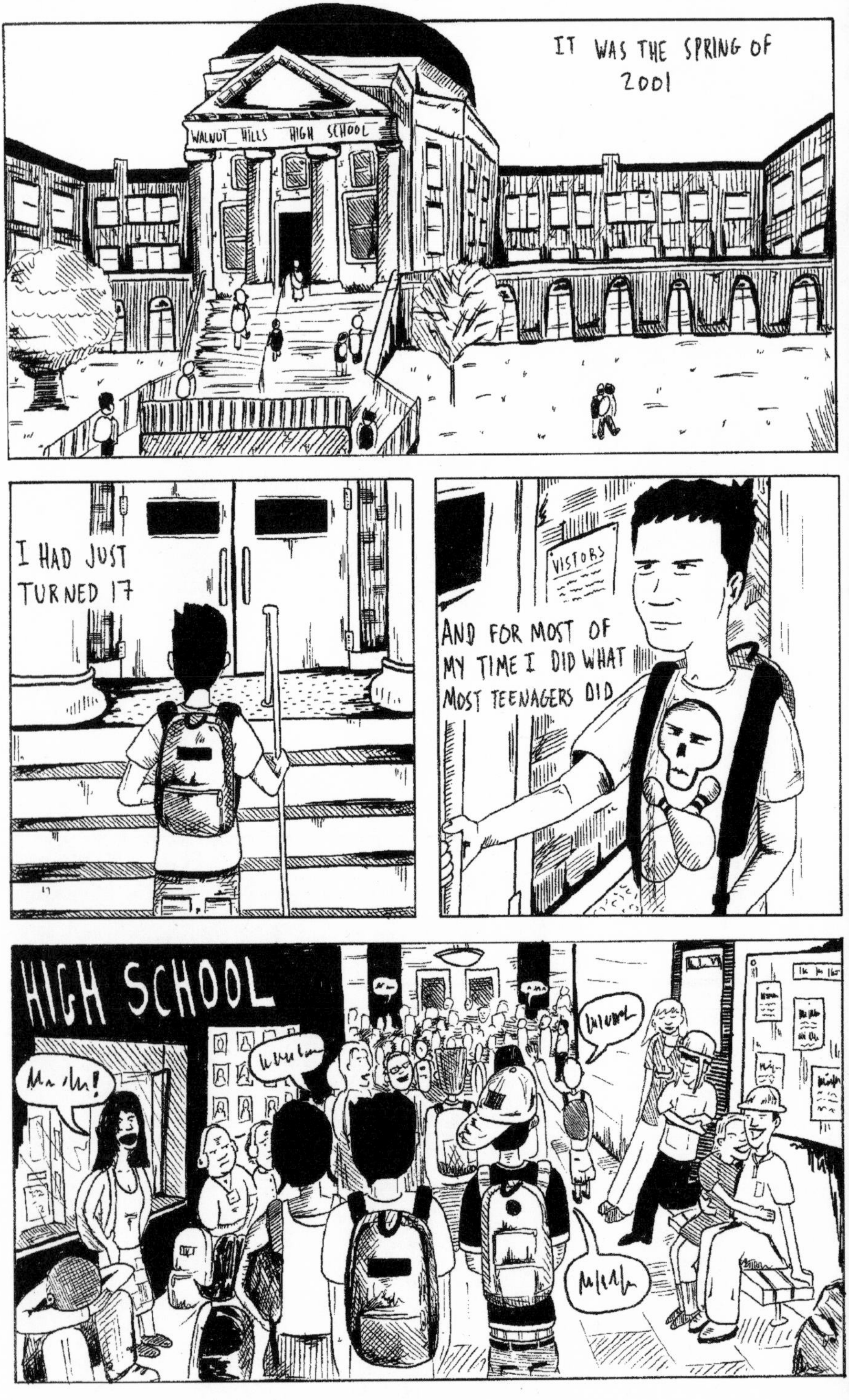
IT WAS THE SPRING OF 2001
WALNUT HILLS HIGH SCHOOL
I HAD JUST TURNED 17
VISTORS
AND FOR MOST OF MY TIME I DID WHAT MOST TEENAGERS DID
HIGH SCHOOL

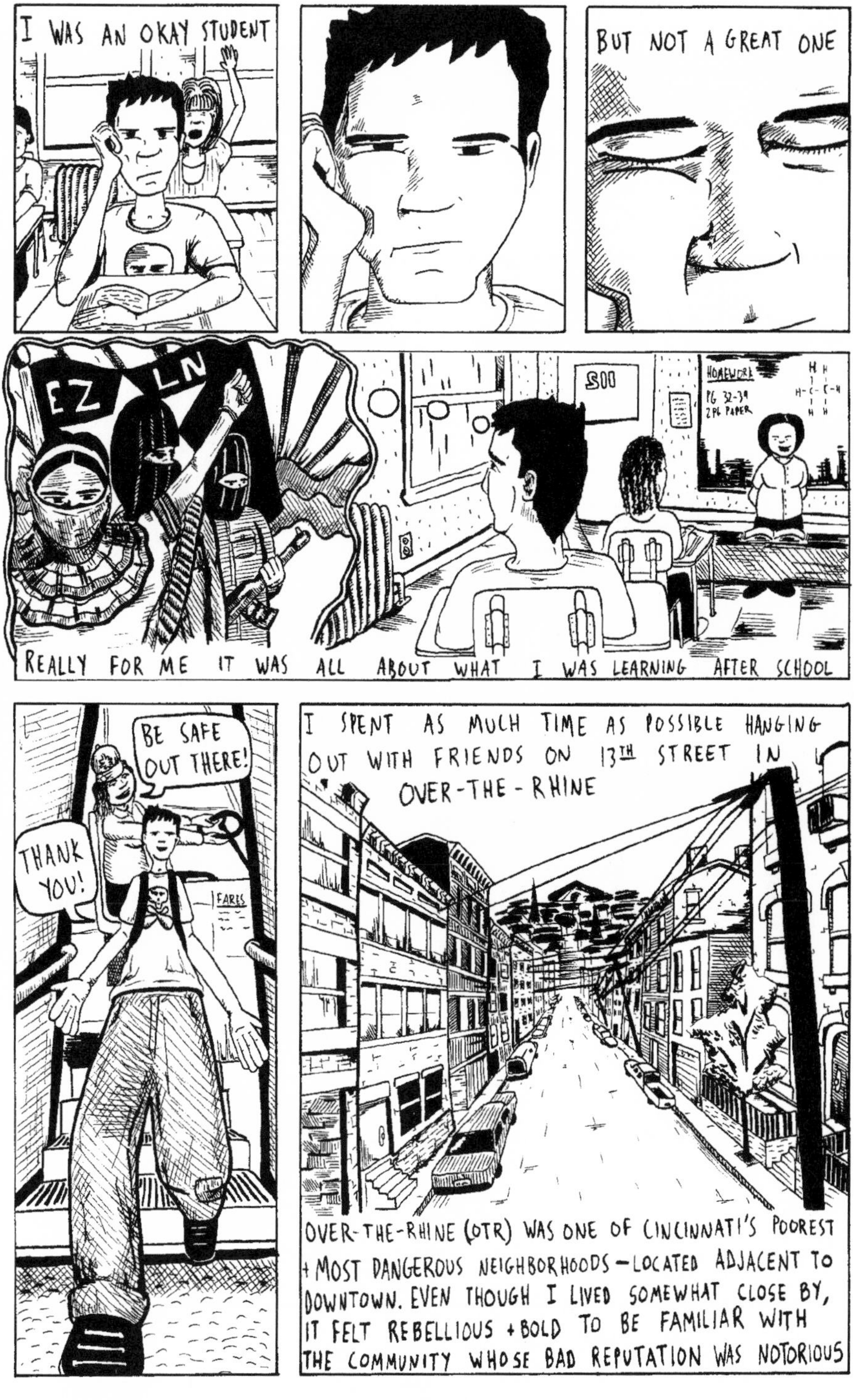
I WAS AN OKAY STUDENT
BUT NOT A GREAT ONE
EZ LN
S00
HOMEWORK
PG 32-39
2PG PAPER
REALLY FOR ME IT WAS ALL ABOUT WHAT I WAS LEARNING AFTER SCHOOL
BE SAFE OUT THERE!
THANK YOU!
FARES
I SPENT AS MUCH TIME AS POSSIBLE HANGING OUT WITH FRIENDS ON 13TH STREET IN OVER-THE-RHINE
OVER-THE-RHINE (OTR) WAS ONE OF CINCINNATI'S POOREST + MOST DANGEROUS NEIGHBORHOODS — LOCATED ADJACENT TO DOWNTOWN. EVEN THOUGH I LIVED SOMEWHAT CLOSE BY, IT FELT REBELLIOUS + BOLD TO BE FAMILIAR WITH THE COMMUNITY WHOSE BAD REPUTATION WAS NOTORIOUS

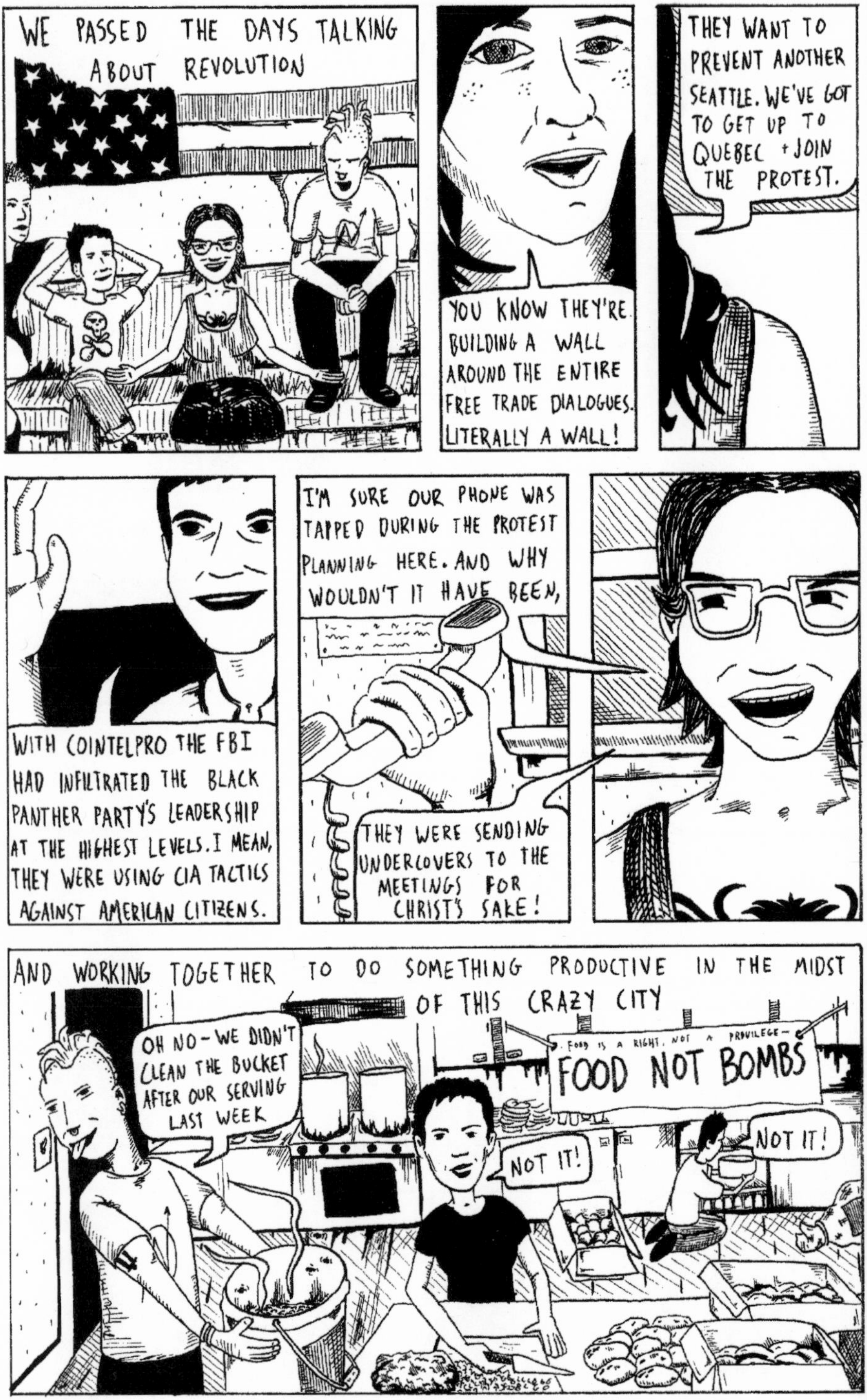
WE PASSED THE DAYS TALKING ABOUT REVOLUTION
YOU KNOW THEY'RE BUILDING A WALL AROUND THE ENTIRE FREE TRADE DIALOGUES. LITERALLY A WALL!
THEY WANT TO PREVENT ANOTHER SEATTLE. WE'VE GOT TO GET UP TO QUEBEC + JOIN THE PROTEST.
WITH COINTELPRO THE FBI HAD INFILTRATED THE BLACK PANTHER PARTY'S LEADERSHIP AT THE HIGHEST LEVELS. I MEAN, THEY WERE USING CIA TACTICS AGAINST AMERICAN CITIZENS.
I'M SURE OUR PHONE WAS TAPPED DURING THE PROTEST PLANNING HERE. AND WHY WOULDN'T IT HAVE BEEN,
THEY WERE SENDING UNDERCOVERS TO THE MEETINGS FOR CHRIST'S SAKE!
AND WORKING TOGETHER TO DO SOMETHING PRODUCTIVE IN THE MIDST OF THIS CRAZY CITY
OH NO - WE DIDN'T CLEAN THE BUCKET AFTER OUR SERVING LAST WEEK
FOOD IS A RIGHT, NOT A PRIVILEGE - FOOD NOT BOMBS
NOT IT!
NOT IT!

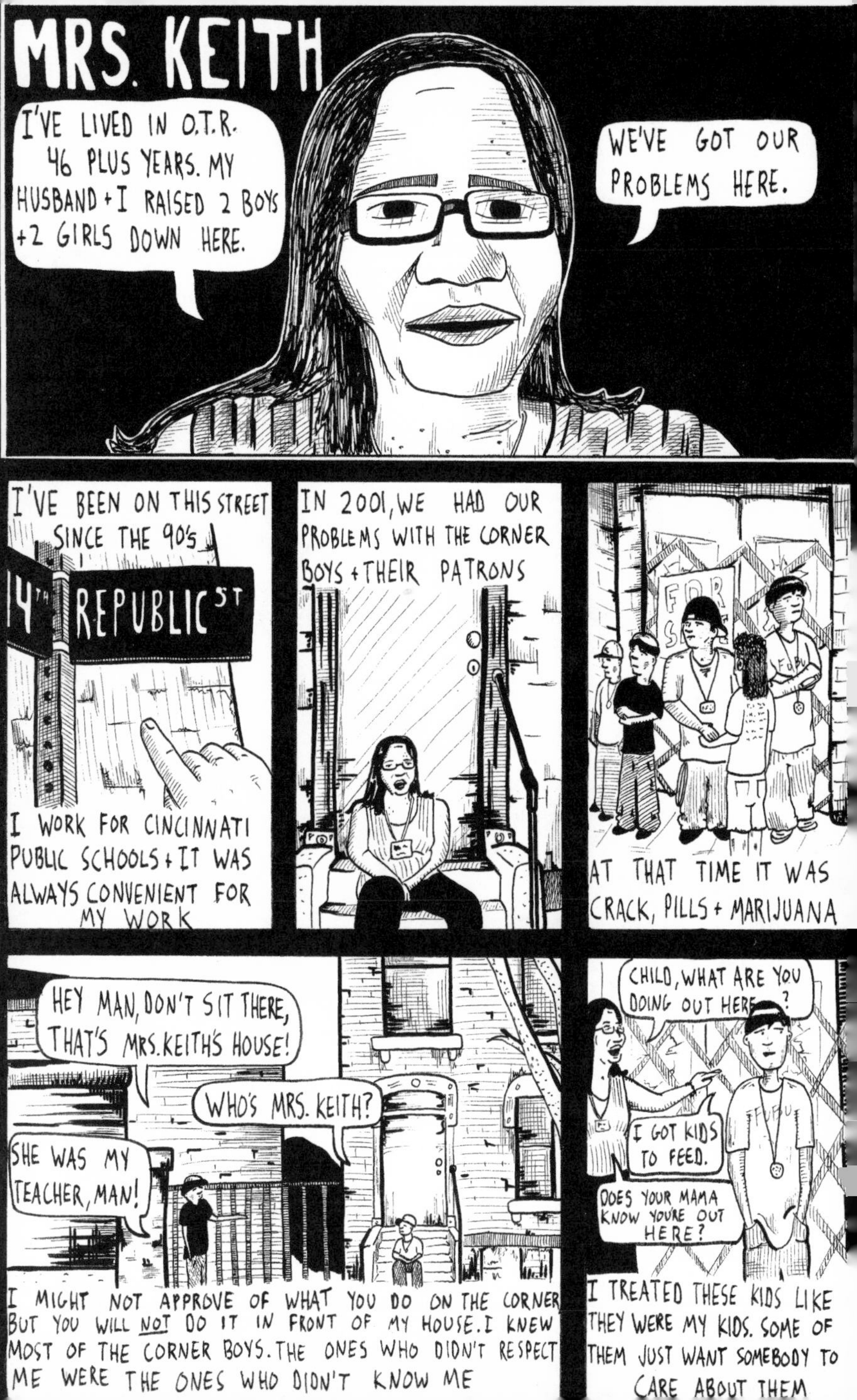

MRS. KEITH
I'VE LIVED IN O.T.R. 46 PLUS YEARS. MY HUSBAND + I RAISED 2 BOYS + 2 GIRLS DOWN HERE.
WE'VE GOT OUR PROBLEMS HERE.
I'VE BEEN ON THIS STREET SINCE THE 90'S
14TH
REPUBLIC ST
I WORK FOR CINCINNATI PUBLIC SCHOOLS + IT WAS ALWAYS CONVENIENT FOR MY WORK
IN 2001, WE HAD OUR PROBLEMS WITH THE CORNER BOYS + THEIR PATRONS
AT THAT TIME IT WAS CRACK, PILLS + MARIJUANA
HEY MAN, DON'T SIT THERE, THAT'S MRS. KEITH'S HOUSE!
WHO'S MRS. KEITH?
SHE WAS MY TEACHER, MAN!
I MIGHT NOT APPROVE OF WHAT YOU DO ON THE CORNER BUT YOU WILL NOT DO IT IN FRONT OF MY HOUSE. I KNEW MOST OF THE CORNER BOYS. THE ONES WHO DIDN'T RESPECT ME WERE THE ONES WHO DIDN'T KNOW ME
CHILD, WHAT ARE YOU DOING OUT HERE ?
I GOT KIDS TO FEED.
DOES YOUR MAMA KNOW YOU'RE OUT HERE?
I TREATED THESE KIDS LIKE THEY WERE MY KIDS. SOME OF THEM JUST WANT SOMEBODY TO CARE ABOUT THEM

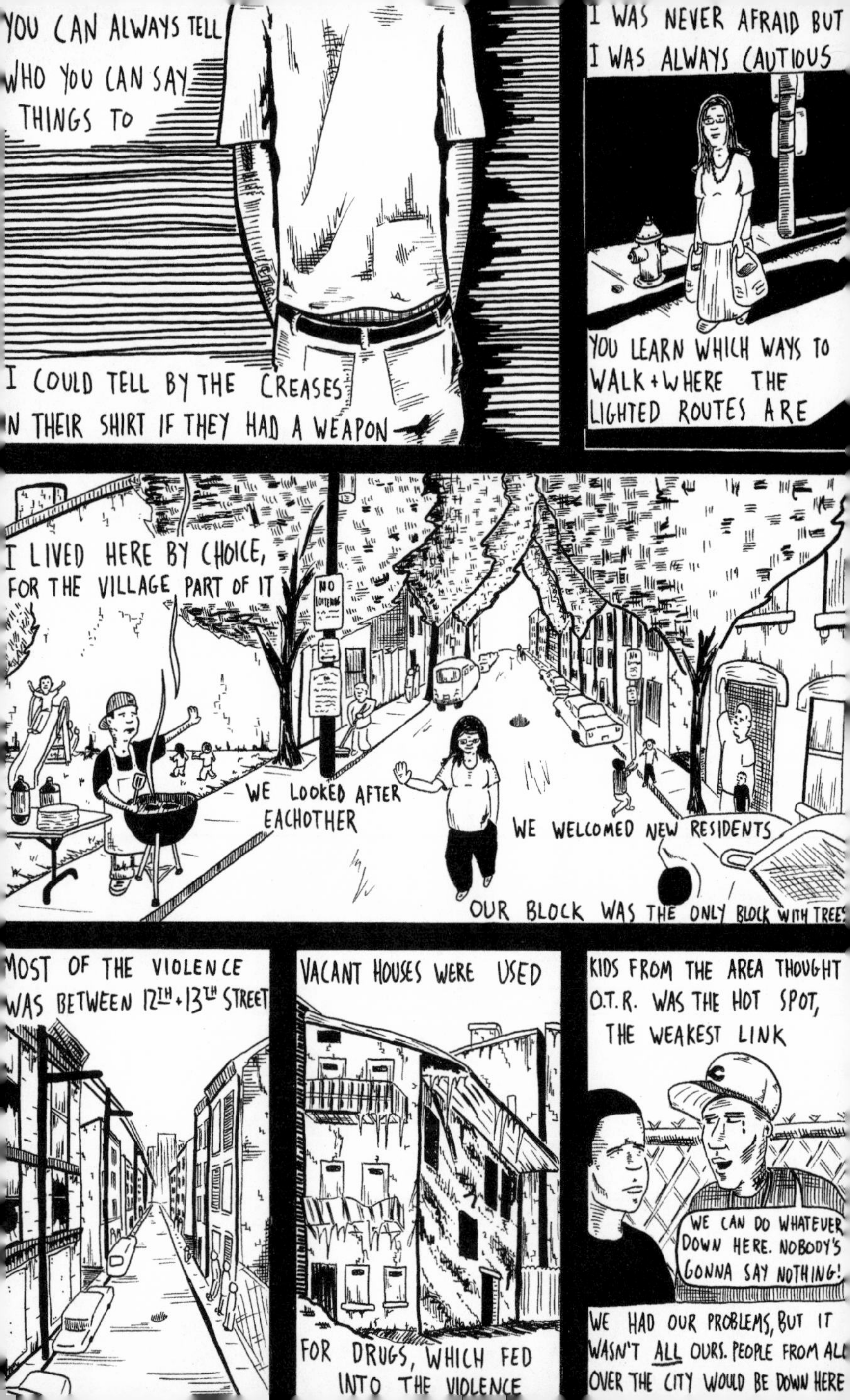
YOU CAN ALWAYS TELL WHO YOU CAN SAY THINGS TO
I COULD TELL BY THE CREASES IN THEIR SHIRT IF THEY HAD A WEAPON
I WAS NEVER AFRAID BUT I WAS ALWAYS CAUTIOUS
YOU LEARN WHICH WAYS TO WALK + WHERE THE LIGHTED ROUTES ARE
I LIVED HERE BY CHOICE, FOR THE VILLAGE PART OF IT
NO LOITERING
WE LOOKED AFTER EACHOTHER
WE WELCOMED NEW RESIDENTS
OUR BLOCK WAS THE ONLY BLOCK WITH TREES
MOST OF THE VIOLENCE WAS BETWEEN 12TH + 13TH STREET
VACANT HOUSES WERE USED
FOR DRUGS, WHICH FED INTO THE VIOLENCE
KIDS FROM THE AREA THOUGHT O.T.R. WAS THE HOT SPOT, THE WEAKEST LINK
WE CAN DO WHATEVER DOWN HERE. NOBODY'S GONNA SAY NOTHING!
WE HAD OUR PROBLEMS, BUT IT WASN'T ALL OURS. PEOPLE FROM ALL OVER THE CITY WOULD BE DOWN HERE

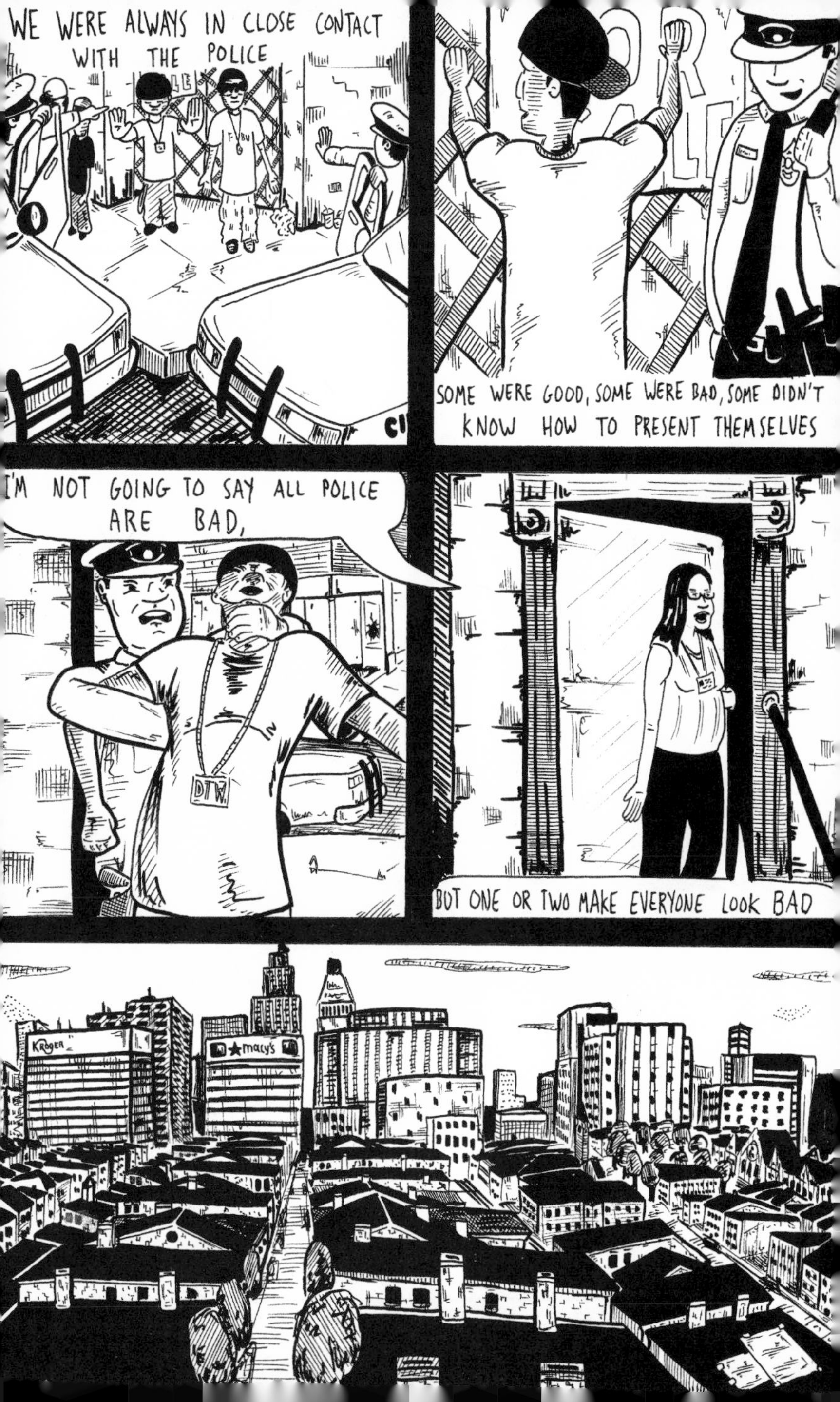
WE WERE ALWAYS IN CLOSE CONTACT WITH THE POLICE
SOME WERE GOOD, SOME WERE BAD, SOME DIDN'T KNOW HOW TO PRESENT THEMSELVES
I'M NOT GOING TO SAY ALL POLICE ARE BAD,
BUT ONE OR TWO MAKE EVERYONE LOOK BAD
DTW.
KROGER
macy's

ONE SUNDAY WE DISRUPTED A PHOTO SHOOT DOWNTOWN TO PROTEST AGAINST HOMELESSNESS

STOP CORPORATE WELFARE!

WE GOT BOOTED OUT + WALKED BACK TO O.T.R.

I CAN'T BELIEVE WE JUST DID THAT!

MY HEART IS STILL POUNDING.

HA HA HA

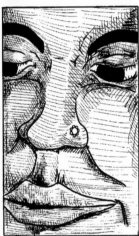

HA HA...

WHAT ARE YOU CLEANING THIS LOT FOR?

TO PAY OUR RESPECTS...

...POLICE KILLED A YOUNG MAN HERE LAST NIGHT.

12

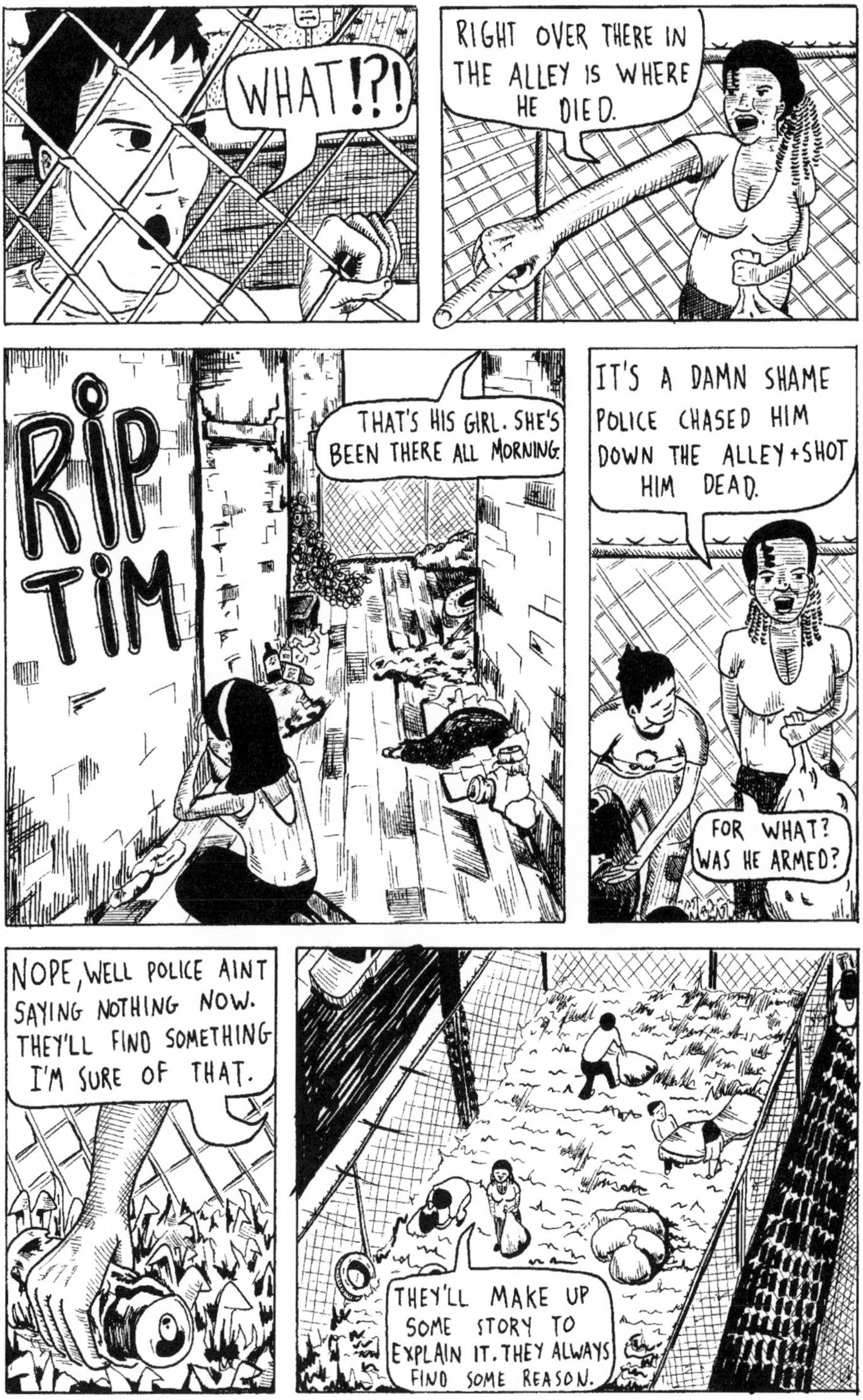
WHAT!?!
RIGHT OVER THERE IN THE ALLEY IS WHERE HE DIED.
RIP TIM
THAT'S HIS GIRL. SHE'S BEEN THERE ALL MORNING.
IT'S A DAMN SHAME POLICE CHASED HIM DOWN THE ALLEY + SHOT HIM DEAD.
FOR WHAT? WAS HE ARMED?
NOPE, WELL POLICE AINT SAYING NOTHING NOW. THEY'LL FIND SOMETHING I'M SURE OF THAT.
THEY'LL MAKE UP SOME STORY TO EXPLAIN IT. THEY ALWAYS FIND SOME REASON.

Y'ALL FROM THE T.A.B.D.

WELL...WE PROTESTED AGAINST IT.

A FEW MONTHS EARLIER, IN NOV. 2000, THOUSANDS OF PROTESTERS DEMONSTRATED AGAINST THE TRANS-ATLANTIC BUSINESS DIALOGUE (TABD) OVER THE COURSE OF SEVERAL DAYS

Talking About Buying-off Democracy

CHIQUITA

FREE TRADE BAD FOR ENVIRONAUT

PROCTER + GAMBLE

PEOPLE OVER PROFIT

IT WAS A MEETING WHERE CEO's + POLITICIANS CAME TO TALK STRATEGY

WELCOME

AND A PLACE WHERE THE ENERGIZED + CONFIDENT ANTI-CORPORATE GLOBALIZATION MOVEMENT CAME TO DISRUPT

THE CINCINNATI POLICE, UNACCUSTOMED TO PROTESTS, WERE HEAVY-HANDED

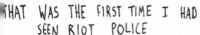
THAT WAS THE FIRST TIME I HAD SEEN RIOT POLICE

A NUMBER OF FRIENDS OF MINE WERE ARRESTED

ONE DAY, DURING THE PROTESTS, THERE WAS A MARCH DUBBED THE "PLEASE DON'T BEAT ME MARCH"

JUSTICE FOR ROGER OWENSBY

ROGER OWENSBY:
A 29 YEAR OLD BLACK MAN WITH A 9 YEAR OLD DAUGHTER WHO HAD DONE 9 YEARS OF MILITARY SERVICE

HE WAS OUT LATE ONE NIGHT IN MADISONVILLE, A DIVERSE WORKING CLASS COMMUNITY, WHEN HE WAS MISIDENTIFIED BY AN OFFICER, CHASED, TACKLED, HANDCUFFED AND THEN MACED, STRUCK + CHOKED

WHILE IN THE SQUAD CAR + CUFFED, ROGER OWENSBY DIED

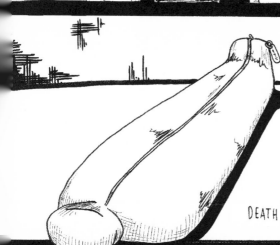

THE CORONER RULED THE DEATH TO BE BY "ASPHYXIATION"

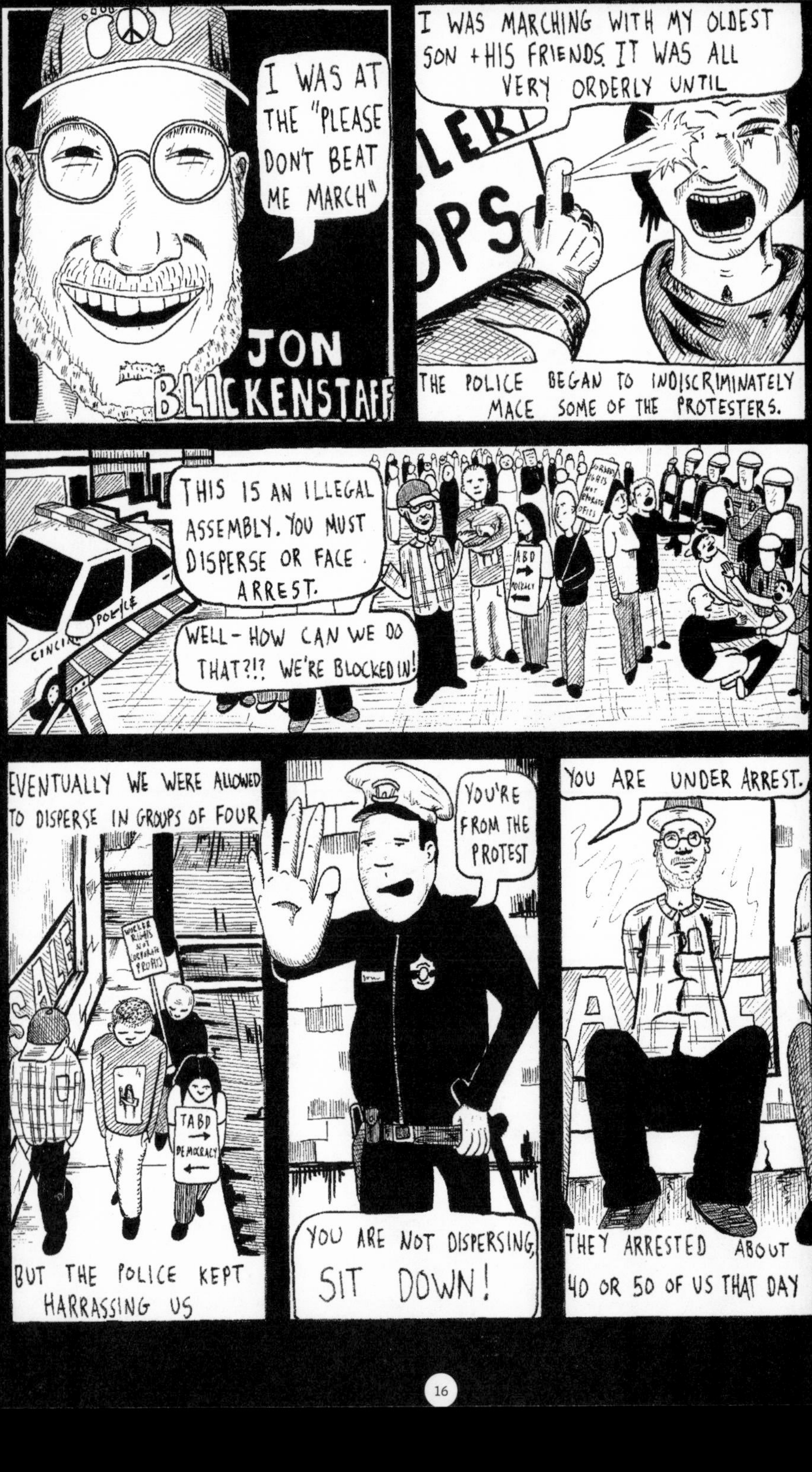
I WAS AT THE "PLEASE DON'T BEAT ME MARCH"
JON BLICKENSTAFF
I WAS MARCHING WITH MY OLDEST SON + HIS FRIENDS. IT WAS ALL VERY ORDERLY UNTIL
THE POLICE BEGAN TO INDISCRIMINATELY MACE SOME OF THE PROTESTERS.
THIS IS AN ILLEGAL ASSEMBLY. YOU MUST DISPERSE OR FACE ARREST.
WELL- HOW CAN WE DO THAT?!? WE'RE BLOCKED IN!
POLICE
EVENTUALLY WE WERE ALLOWED TO DISPERSE IN GROUPS OF FOUR
WORKER RIGHTS NOT CORPORATE PROFITS
TABD → DEMOCRACY ←
BUT THE POLICE KEPT HARRASSING US
YOU'RE FROM THE PROTEST
YOU ARE NOT DISPERSING, SIT DOWN!
YOU ARE UNDER ARREST.
THEY ARRESTED ABOUT 40 OR 50 OF US THAT DAY

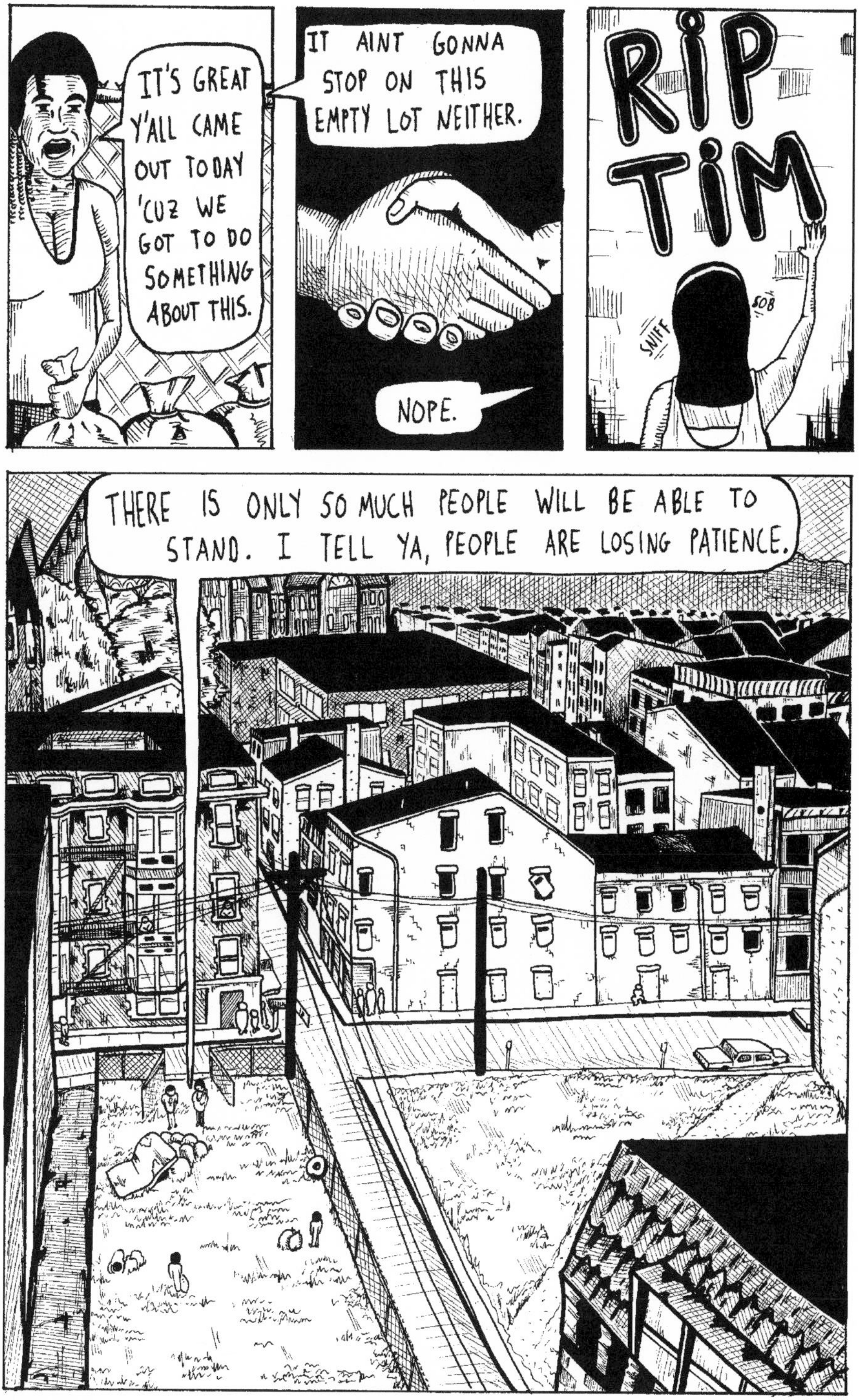
IT'S GREAT Y'ALL CAME OUT TODAY 'CUZ WE GOT TO DO SOMETHING ABOUT THIS.
IT AINT GONNA STOP ON THIS EMPTY LOT NEITHER.
NOPE.
RIP TIM
SNIFF
SOB
THERE IS ONLY SO MUCH PEOPLE WILL BE ABLE TO STAND. I TELL YA, PEOPLE ARE LOSING PATIENCE.

MONDAY

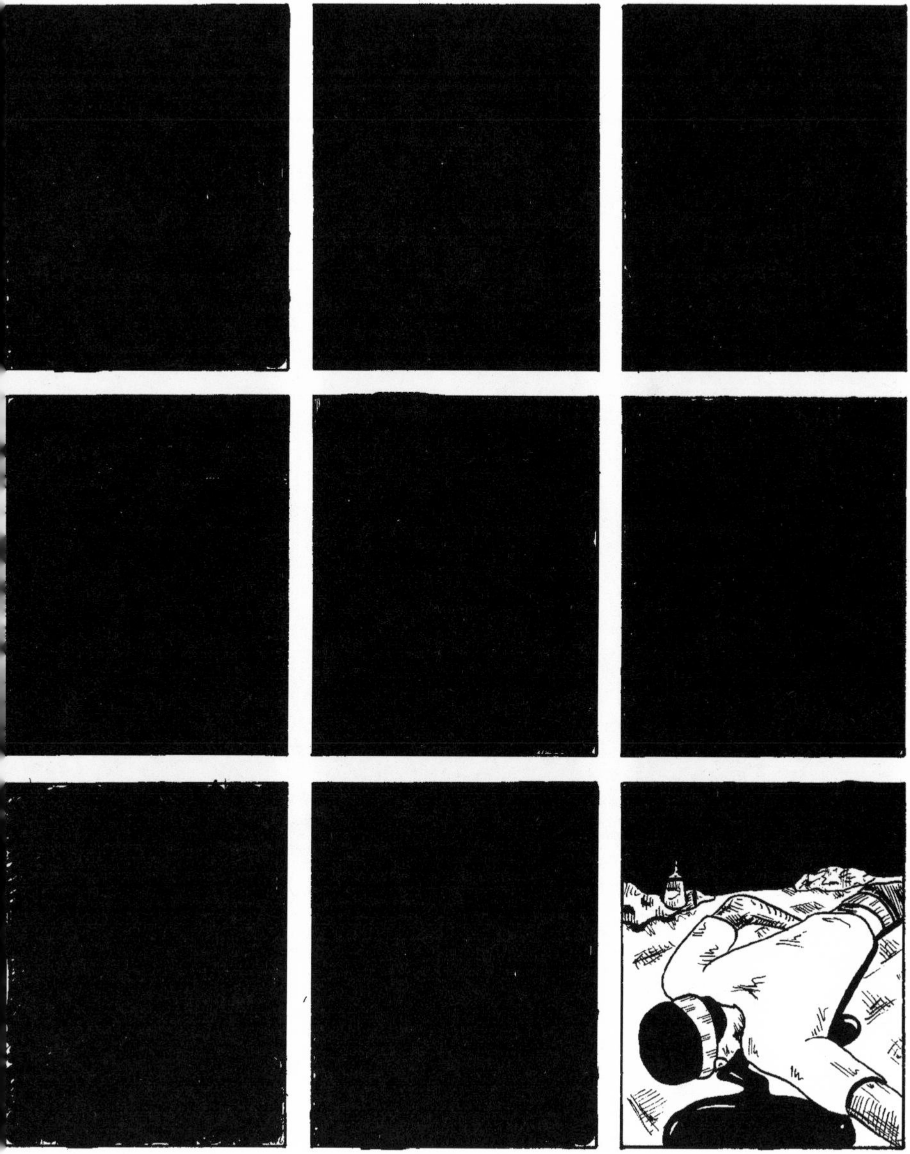

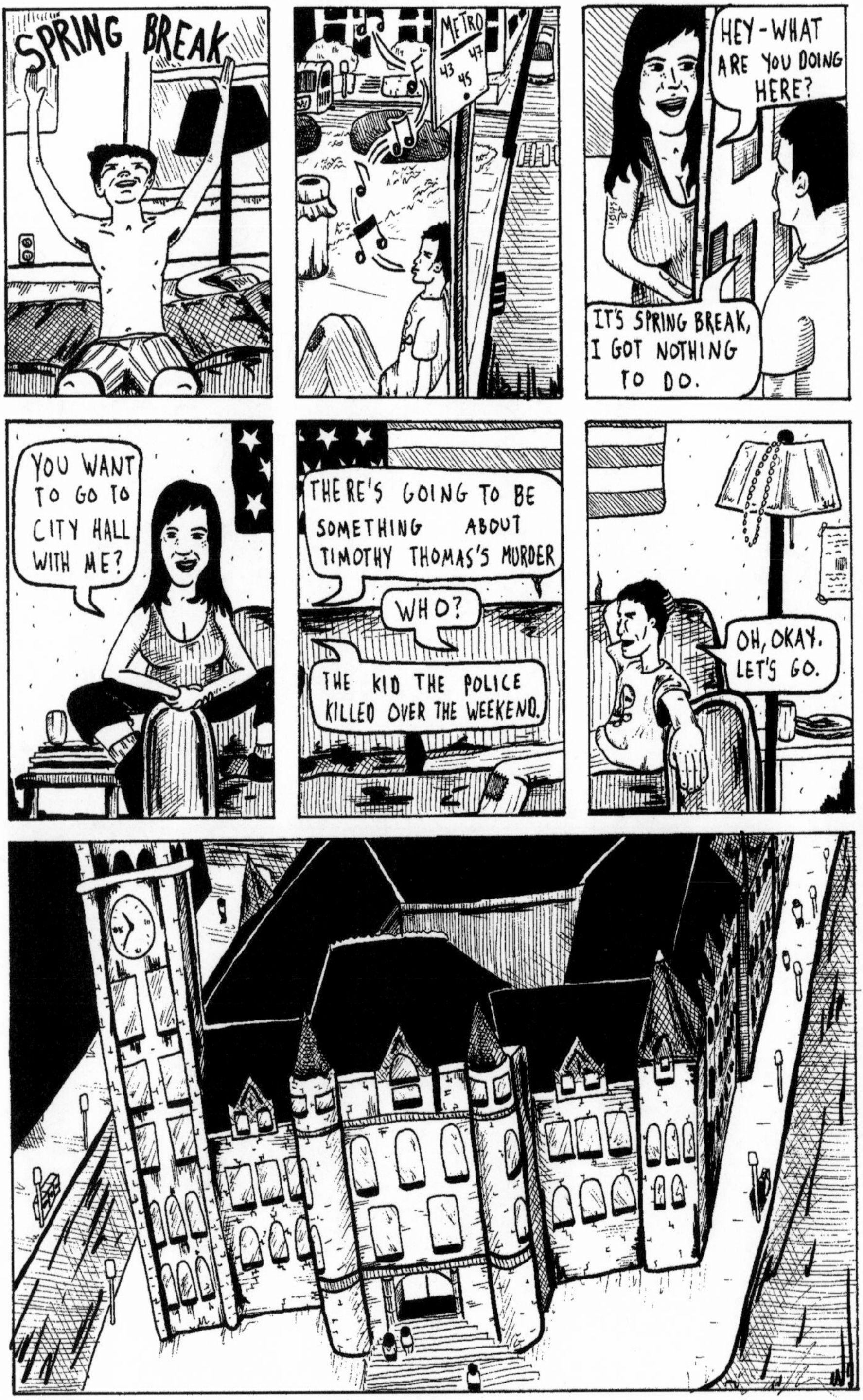
SPRING BREAK
METRO
43
45
47
HEY-WHAT ARE YOU DOING HERE?
IT'S SPRING BREAK, I GOT NOTHING TO DO.
YOU WANT TO GO TO CITY HALL WITH ME?
THERE'S GOING TO BE SOMETHING ABOUT TIMOTHY THOMAS'S MURDER
WHO?
THE KID THE POLICE KILLED OVER THE WEEKEND.
OH, OKAY. LET'S GO.

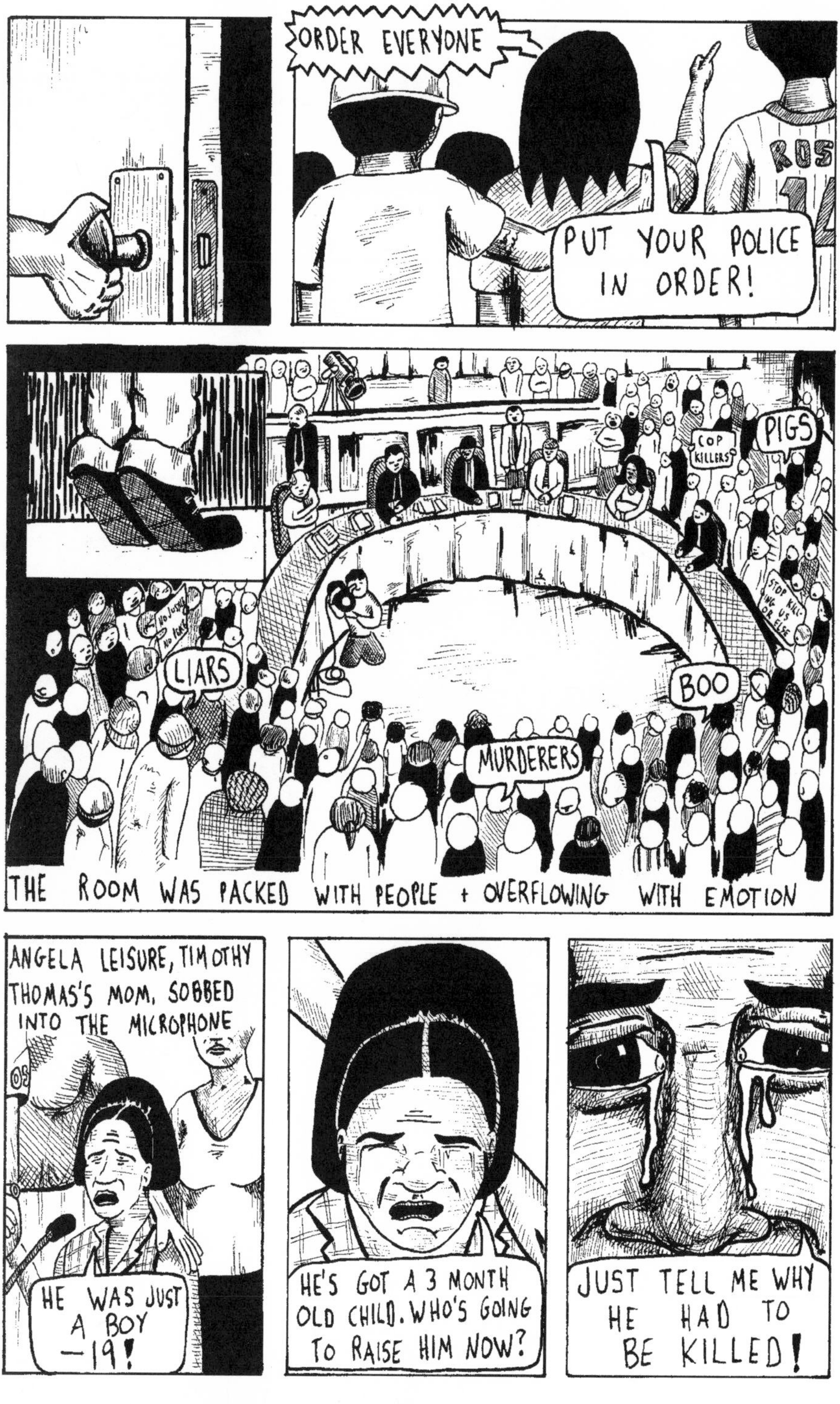
ORDER EVERYONE
PUT YOUR POLICE IN ORDER!
RO5 14
PIGS
COP KILLERS
LIARS
BOO
MURDERERS
THE ROOM WAS PACKED WITH PEOPLE + OVERFLOWING WITH EMOTION
ANGELA LEISURE, TIMOTHY THOMAS'S MOM, SOBBED INTO THE MICROPHONE
HE WAS JUST A BOY —19!
HE'S GOT A 3 MONTH OLD CHILD. WHO'S GOING TO RAISE HIM NOW?
JUST TELL ME WHY HE HAD TO BE KILLED!

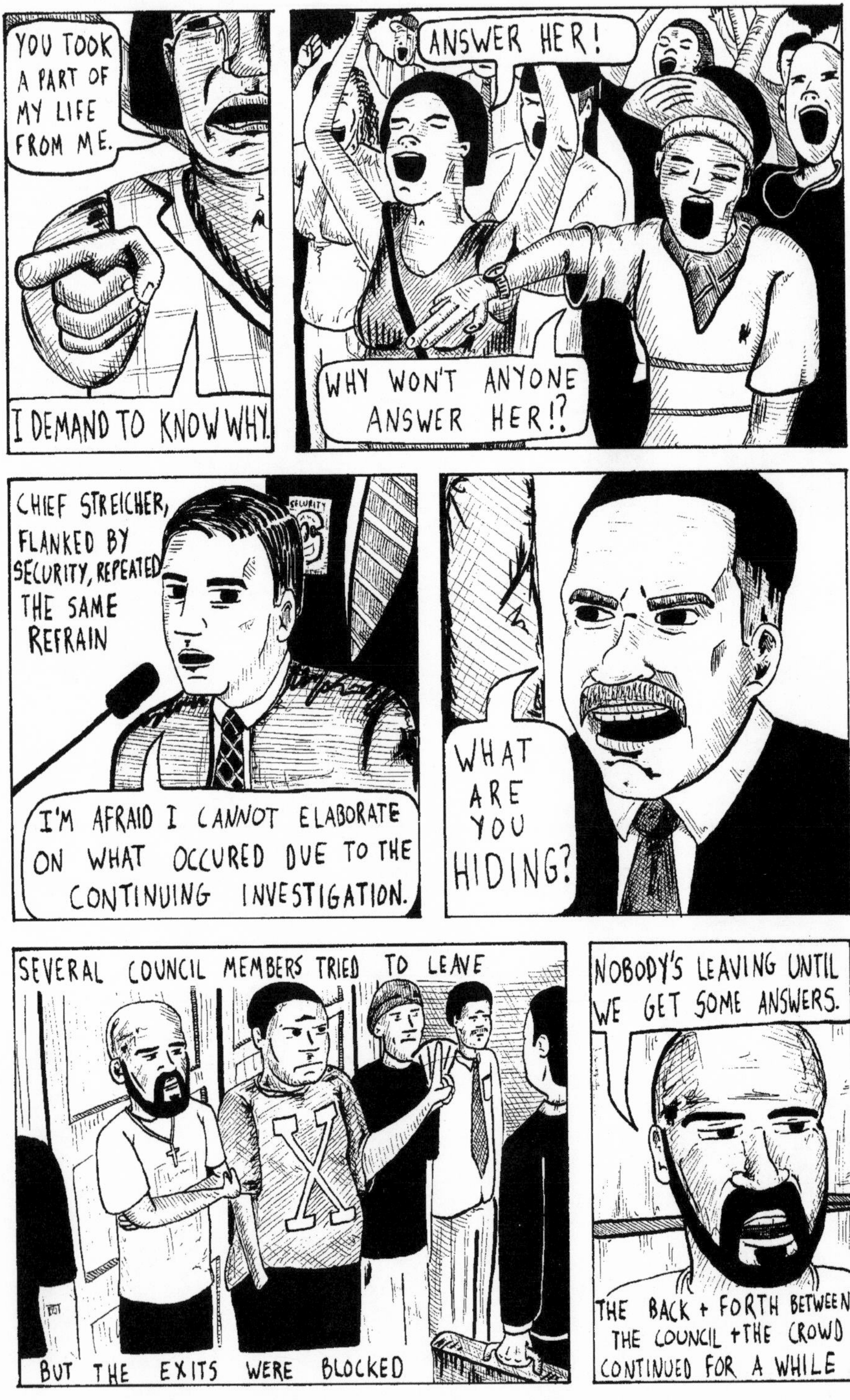
YOU TOOK A PART OF MY LIFE FROM ME.
I DEMAND TO KNOW WHY.
ANSWER HER!
WHY WON'T ANYONE ANSWER HER!?
CHIEF STREICHER, FLANKED BY SECURITY, REPEATED THE SAME REFRAIN
SECURITY
I'M AFRAID I CANNOT ELABORATE ON WHAT OCCURED DUE TO THE CONTINUING INVESTIGATION.
WHAT ARE YOU HIDING?
SEVERAL COUNCIL MEMBERS TRIED TO LEAVE
BUT THE EXITS WERE BLOCKED
NOBODY'S LEAVING UNTIL WE GET SOME ANSWERS.
THE BACK + FORTH BETWEEN THE COUNCIL + THE CROWD CONTINUED FOR A WHILE

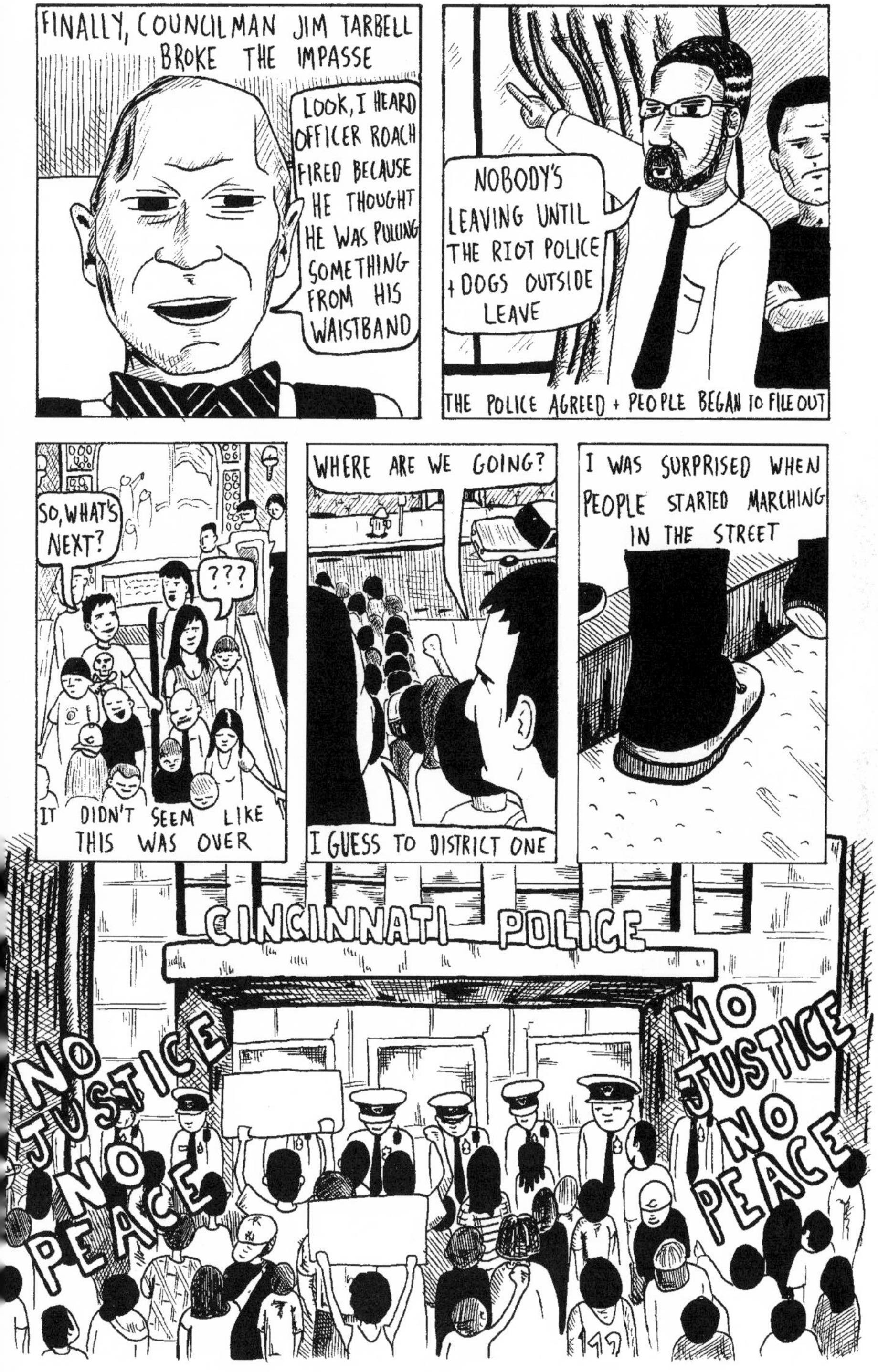
FINALLY, COUNCILMAN JIM TARBELL BROKE THE IMPASSE
LOOK, I HEARD OFFICER ROACH FIRED BECAUSE HE THOUGHT HE WAS PULLING SOMETHING FROM HIS WAISTBAND
NOBODY'S LEAVING UNTIL THE RIOT POLICE + DOGS OUTSIDE LEAVE
THE POLICE AGREED + PEOPLE BEGAN TO FILE OUT
SO, WHAT'S NEXT?
???
IT DIDN'T SEEM LIKE THIS WAS OVER
WHERE ARE WE GOING?
I GUESS TO DISTRICT ONE
I WAS SURPRISED WHEN PEOPLE STARTED MARCHING IN THE STREET
CINCINNATI POLICE
NO JUSTICE NO PEACE
NO JUSTICE NO PEACE

BEFORE THE POLICE CAUGHT UP, A GROUP OF PROTESTERS PULLED DOWN THE FLAG

AND PROCEEDED TO JUMP ON IT

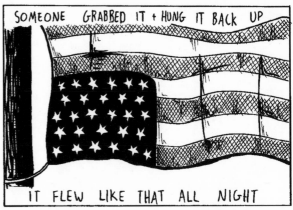

SOMEONE GRABBED IT + HUNG IT BACK UP

IT FLEW LIKE THAT ALL NIGHT

YOU FUCKING MURDERERS! WHY'D YOU KILL HIM!

YA'LL KILLED 15 OF OUR MEN + YOU GOT NO ANSWERS!

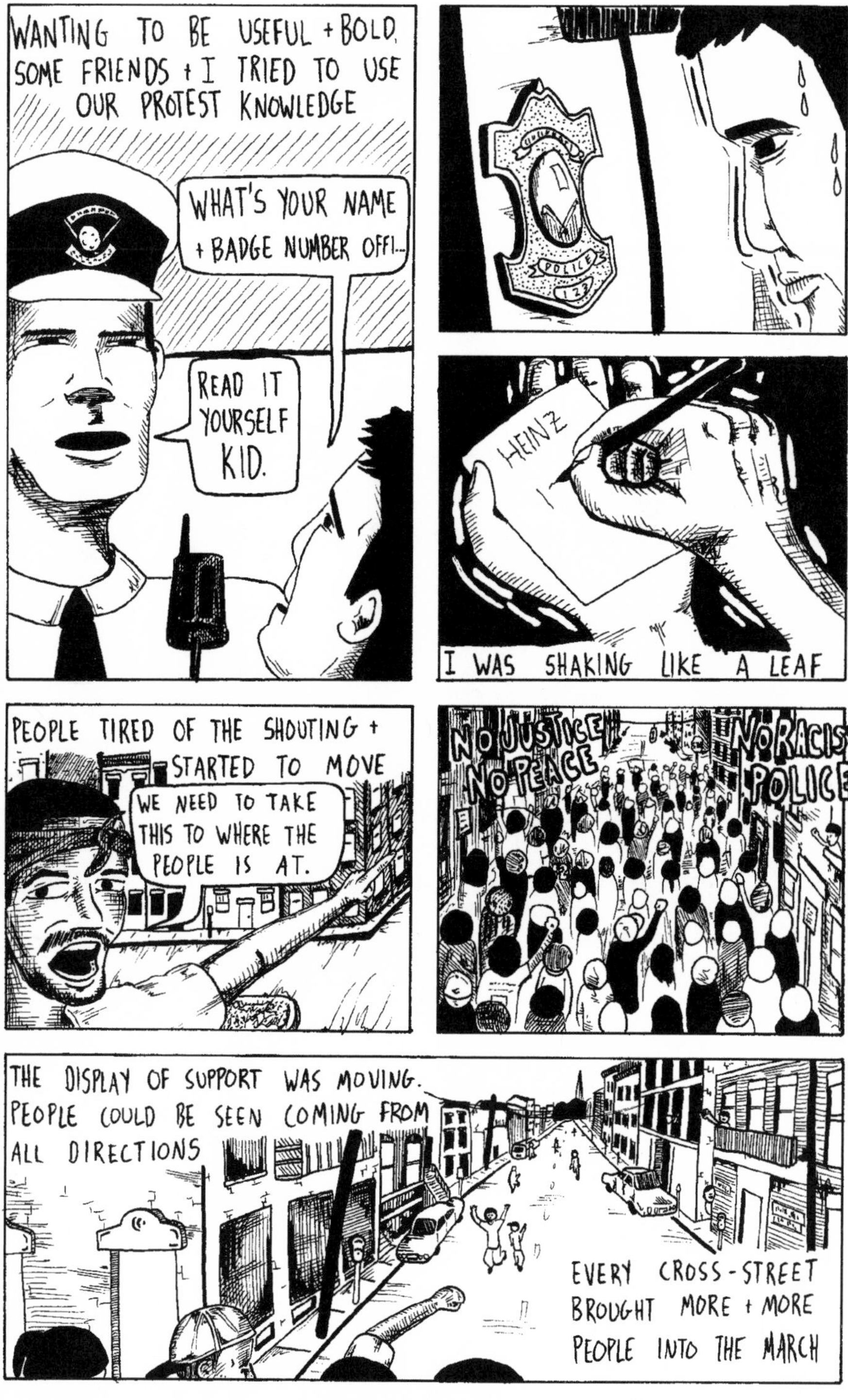
WANTING TO BE USEFUL + BOLD, SOME FRIENDS + I TRIED TO USE OUR PROTEST KNOWLEDGE
WHAT'S YOUR NAME + BADGE NUMBER OFFI...
READ IT YOURSELF KID.
POLICE
123
HEINZ
I WAS SHAKING LIKE A LEAF
PEOPLE TIRED OF THE SHOUTING + STARTED TO MOVE
WE NEED TO TAKE THIS TO WHERE THE PEOPLE IS AT.
NO JUSTICE NO PEACE
NO RACIST POLICE
THE DISPLAY OF SUPPORT WAS MOVING. PEOPLE COULD BE SEEN COMING FROM ALL DIRECTIONS
EVERY CROSS-STREET BROUGHT MORE + MORE PEOPLE INTO THE MARCH

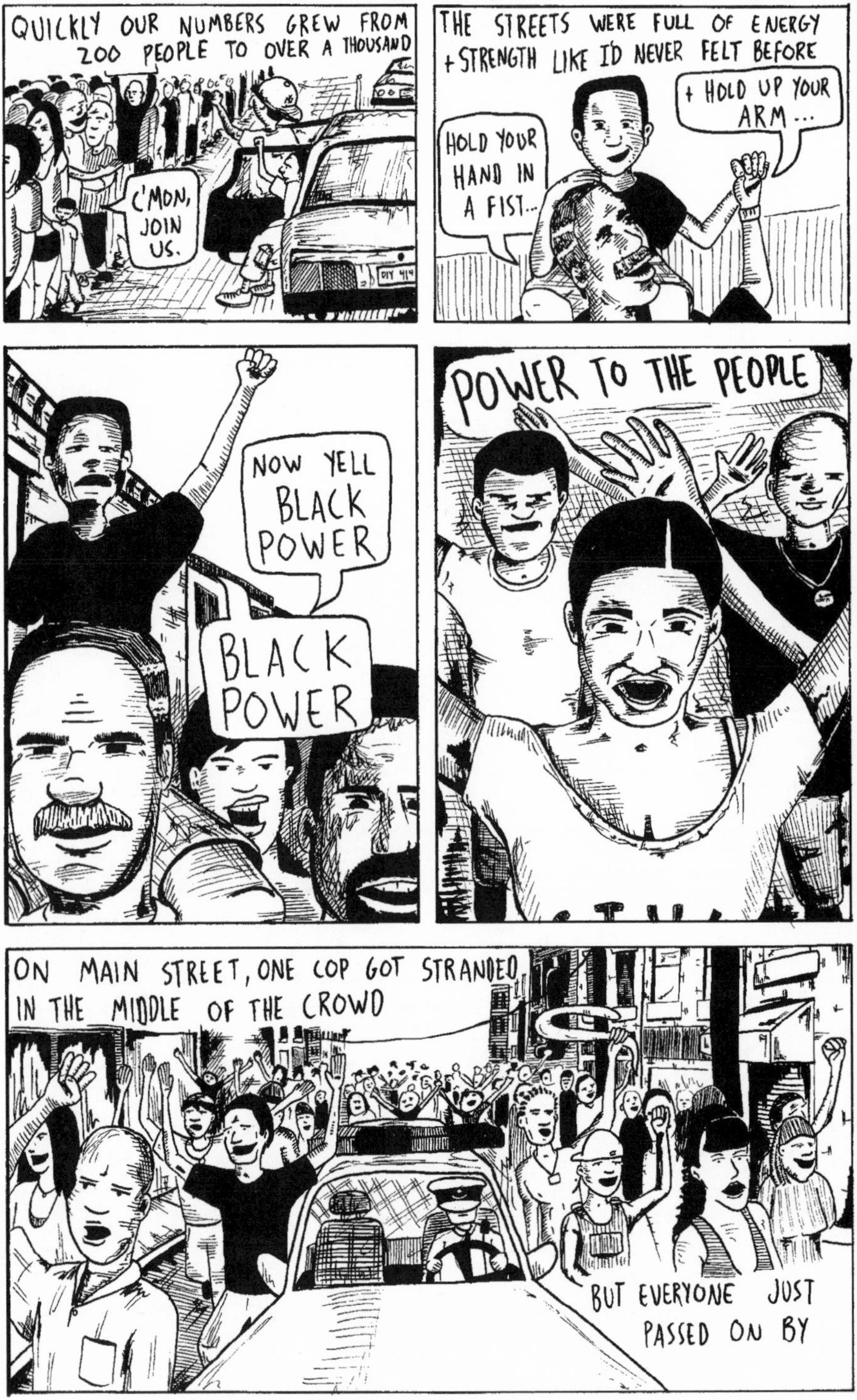
QUICKLY OUR NUMBERS GREW FROM 200 PEOPLE TO OVER A THOUSAND
C'MON, JOIN US.
THE STREETS WERE FULL OF ENERGY + STRENGTH LIKE I'D NEVER FELT BEFORE
HOLD YOUR HAND IN A FIST...
+ HOLD UP YOUR ARM...
NOW YELL BLACK POWER
BLACK POWER
POWER TO THE PEOPLE
ON MAIN STREET, ONE COP GOT STRANDED IN THE MIDDLE OF THE CROWD
BUT EVERYONE JUST PASSED ON BY

UP TO THIS POINT THE POLICE WERE PRETTY HANDS OFF, PROBABLY TO AVOID PROVOKING THE GROWING CROWD

ONCE WE LEFT O.T.R. + WENT TOWARDS DOWNTOWN

IT WAS A DIFFERENT SITUATION

GET BACK!

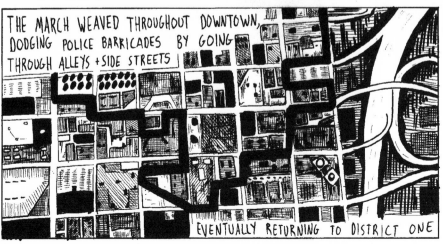

THE MARCH WEAVED THROUGHOUT DOWNTOWN, DODGING POLICE BARRICADES BY GOING THROUGH ALLEYS + SIDE STREETS

EVENTUALLY RETURNING TO DISTRICT ONE

THIS TIME AROUND, THE CROWD WAS MUCH LARGER

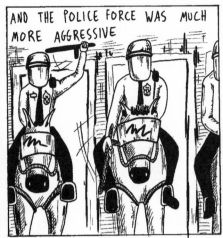

AND THE POLICE FORCE WAS MUCH MORE AGGRESSIVE

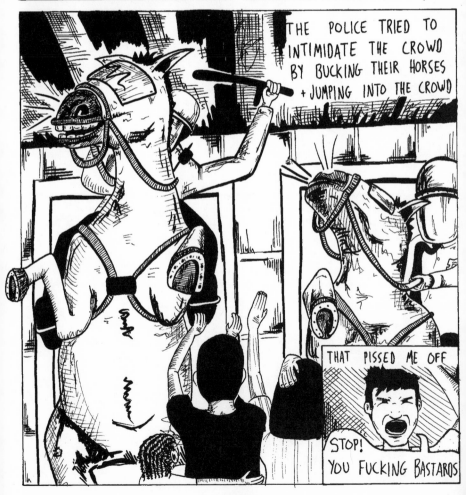

THE POLICE TRIED TO INTIMIDATE THE CROWD BY BUCKING THEIR HORSES + JUMPING INTO THE CROWD

THAT PISSED ME OFF

STOP! YOU FUCKING BASTAROS

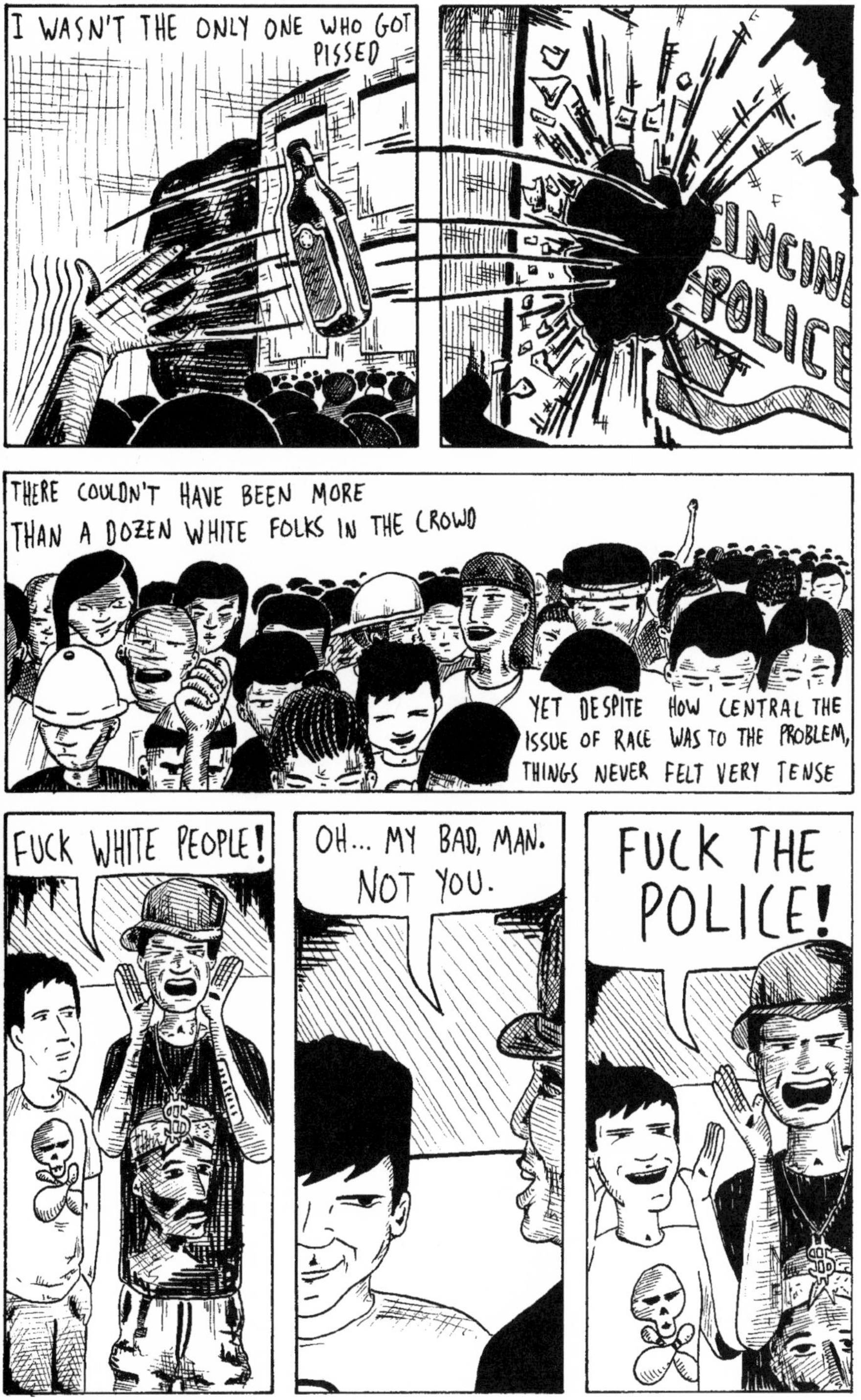
I WASN'T THE ONLY ONE WHO GOT PISSED
POLICE
THERE COULDN'T HAVE BEEN MORE THAN A DOZEN WHITE FOLKS IN THE CROWD
YET DESPITE HOW CENTRAL THE ISSUE OF RACE WAS TO THE PROBLEM, THINGS NEVER FELT VERY TENSE
FUCK WHITE PEOPLE!
OH... MY BAD, MAN. NOT YOU.
FUCK THE POLICE!

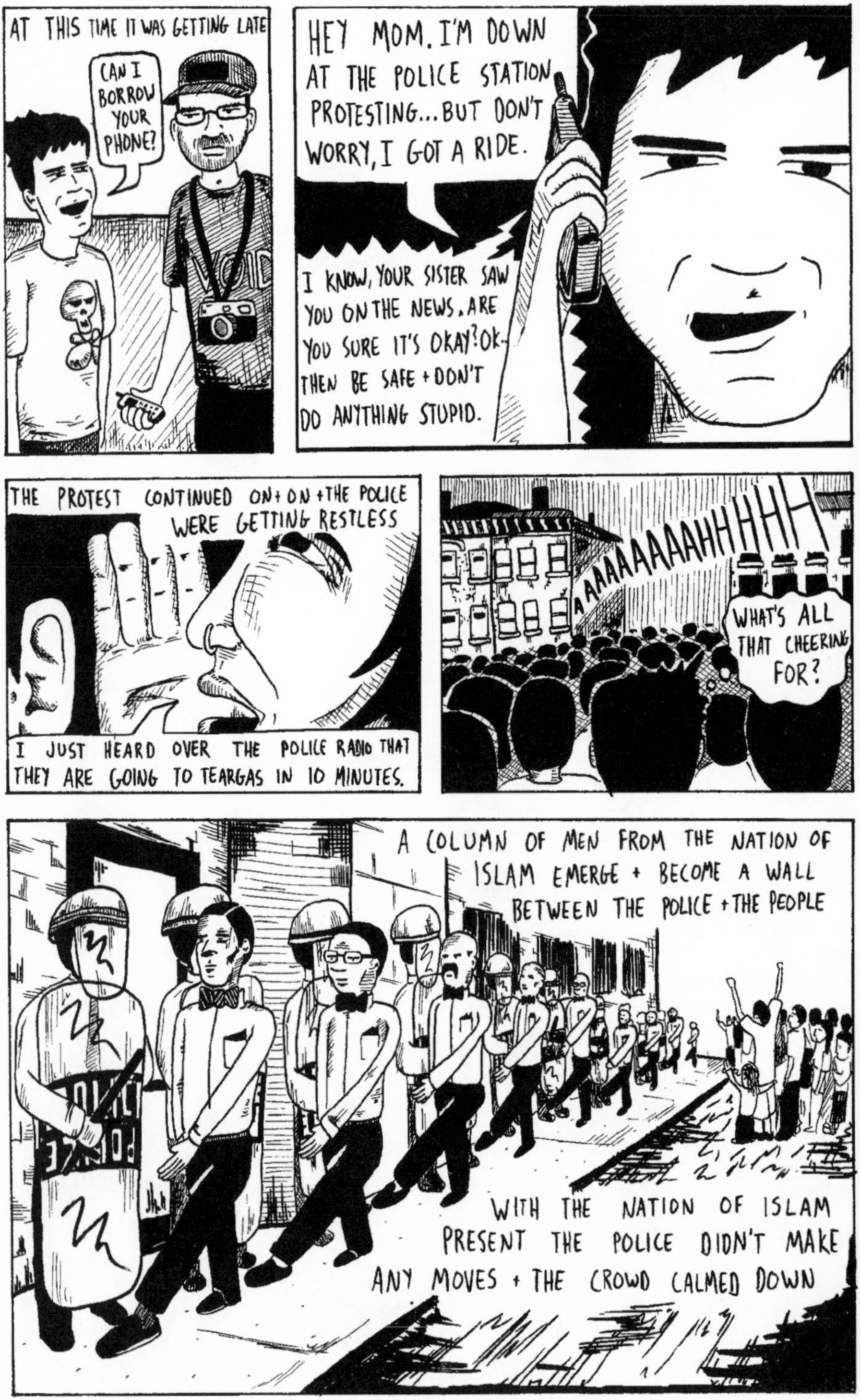
AT THIS TIME IT WAS GETTING LATE
CAN I BORROW YOUR PHONE?
VOID
HEY MOM. I'M DOWN AT THE POLICE STATION PROTESTING... BUT DON'T WORRY, I GOT A RIDE.
I KNOW, YOUR SISTER SAW YOU ON THE NEWS. ARE YOU SURE IT'S OKAY? OK. THEN BE SAFE + DON'T DO ANYTHING STUPID.
THE PROTEST CONTINUED ON + ON + THE POLICE WERE GETTING RESTLESS
I JUST HEARD OVER THE POLICE RADIO THAT THEY ARE GOING TO TEARGAS IN 10 MINUTES.
AAAAAAAAAHHHHHH
WHAT'S ALL THAT CHEERING FOR?
A COLUMN OF MEN FROM THE NATION OF ISLAM EMERGE + BECOME A WALL BETWEEN THE POLICE + THE PEOPLE
POLICE
WITH THE NATION OF ISLAM PRESENT THE POLICE DIDN'T MAKE ANY MOVES + THE CROWD CALMED DOWN

LITTLE BY LITTLE, PEOPLE STARTED TO RECOGNIZE THE MAGNITUDE OF THE DAY

LOOK AROUND PEOPLE! IF WE CAN GET A COUPLE HUNDRED BLACK PEOPLE AND HOLD THE POLICE OFF ALL DAY, IMAGINE WHAT ALL THE BLACK PEOPLE IN THE CITY CAN DO IF WE CAN SQUASH ALL THE BEEFIN' & WORK TOGETHER!

SOMEHOW A CAR GOT INTO THE CROWD + BUMPED THE STEREO

+ A PARTY BEGAN

PEOPLE GOT INTO A GOOFY MOOD

WE SMOKE WEED

WE SMOKE WEED

I FINALLY LEFT WITH MY RIDE AROUND MIDNIGHT

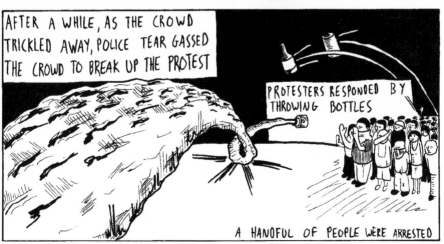

AFTER A WHILE, AS THE CROWD TRICKLED AWAY, POLICE TEAR GASSED THE CROWD TO BREAK UP THE PROTEST

PROTESTERS RESPONDED BY THROWING BOTTLES

A HANDFUL OF PEOPLE WERE ARRESTED

TUESDAY

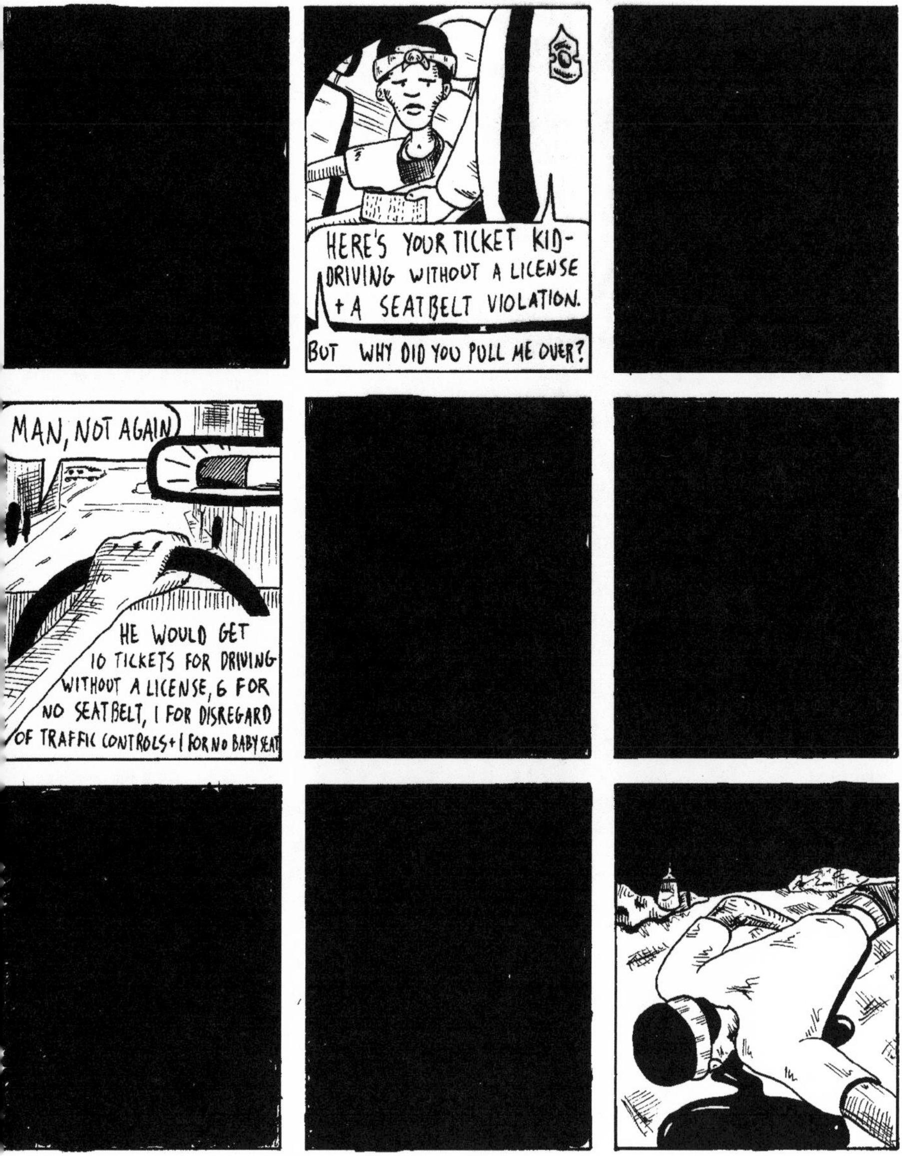
HERE'S YOUR TICKET KID- DRIVING WITHOUT A LICENSE + A SEATBELT VIOLATION.
BUT WHY DID YOU PULL ME OVER?
MAN, NOT AGAIN
HE WOULD GET 10 TICKETS FOR DRIVING WITHOUT A LICENSE, 6 FOR NO SEATBELT, 1 FOR DISREGARD OF TRAFFIC CONTROLS+1 FOR NO BABY SEAT

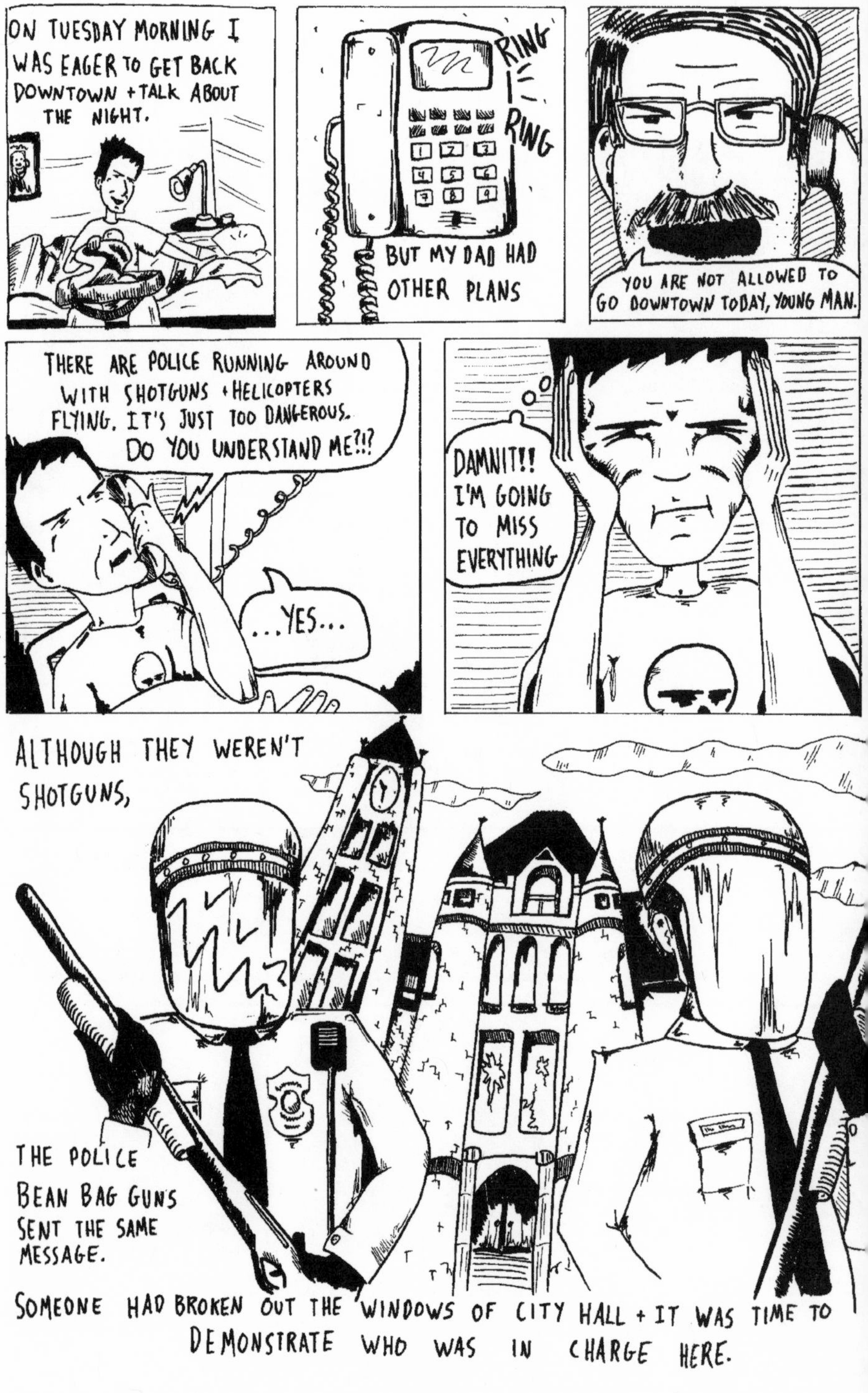
ON TUESDAY MORNING I WAS EAGER TO GET BACK DOWNTOWN + TALK ABOUT THE NIGHT.
RING
RING
BUT MY DAD HAD OTHER PLANS
YOU ARE NOT ALLOWED TO GO DOWNTOWN TODAY, YOUNG MAN.
THERE ARE POLICE RUNNING AROUND WITH SHOTGUNS + HELICOPTERS FLYING. IT'S JUST TOO DANGEROUS. DO YOU UNDERSTAND ME?!?
...YES...
DAMNIT!! I'M GOING TO MISS EVERYTHING
ALTHOUGH THEY WEREN'T SHOTGUNS,
THE POLICE BEAN BAG GUNS SENT THE SAME MESSAGE.
SOMEONE HAD BROKEN OUT THE WINDOWS OF CITY HALL + IT WAS TIME TO DEMONSTRATE WHO WAS IN CHARGE HERE.

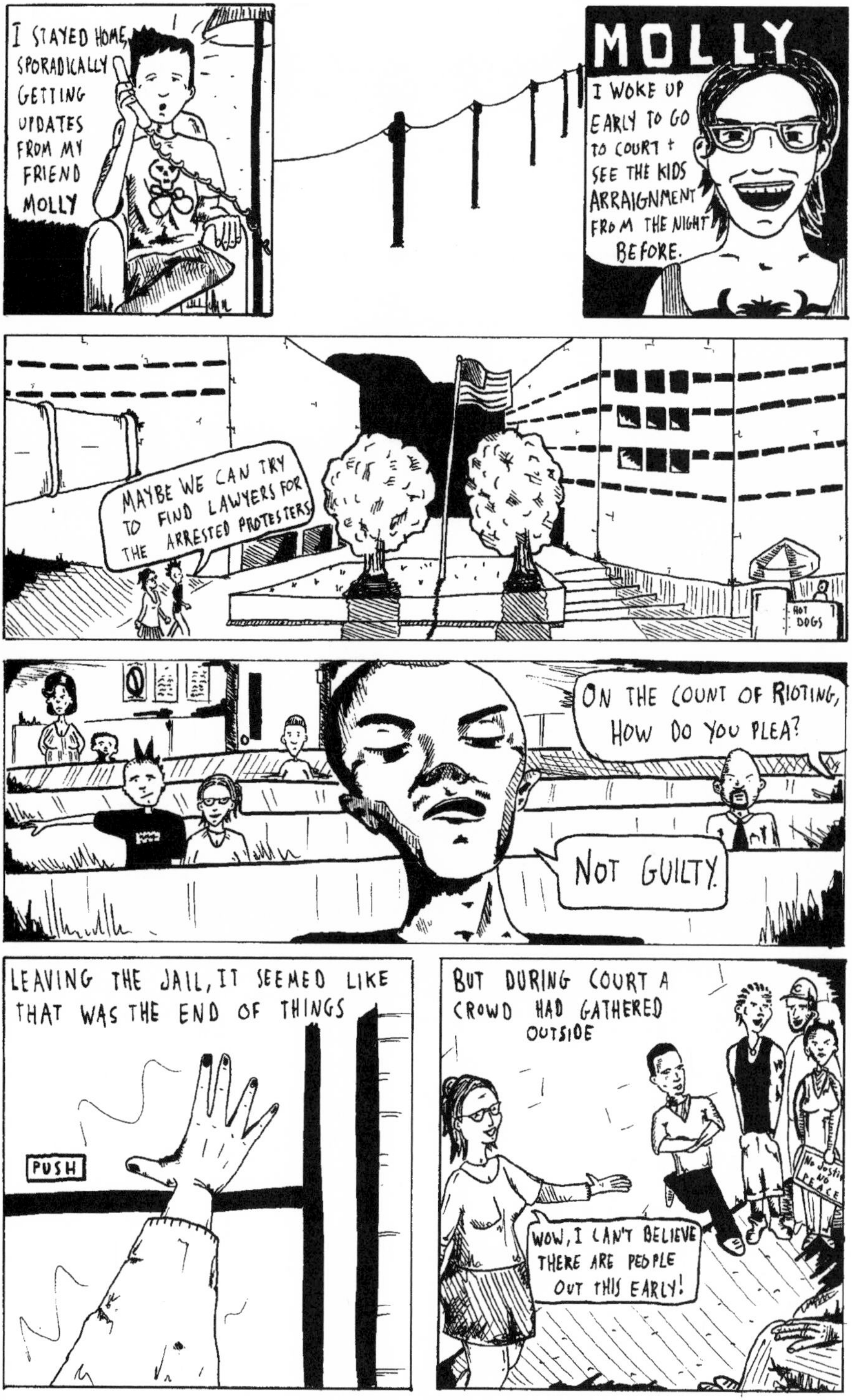
I STAYED HOME, SPORADICALLY GETTING UPDATES FROM MY FRIEND MOLLY
MOLLY
I WOKE UP EARLY TO GO TO COURT + SEE THE KIDS ARRAIGNMENT FROM THE NIGHT BEFORE.
MAYBE WE CAN TRY TO FIND LAWYERS FOR THE ARRESTED PROTESTERS.
HOT DOGS
ON THE COUNT OF RIOTING, HOW DO YOU PLEA?
NOT GUILTY.
LEAVING THE JAIL, IT SEEMED LIKE THAT WAS THE END OF THINGS
PUSH
BUT DURING COURT A CROWD HAD GATHERED OUTSIDE
WOW, I CAN'T BELIEVE THERE ARE PEOPLE OUT THIS EARLY!

THE CROWD GOT MOVING + WORKED ITS WAY THROUGH OVER-THE-RHINE
DON'T SHOOT
NO JUSTICE NO PEACE
PEOPLE WERE FLOODING IN FROM ALL THE SIDE STREETS + THE CROWD QUICKLY SWELLED TO HUNDREDS OF PEOPLE
IT SEEMED LIKE EVERYONE WAS JOINING UP WITH THE MARCH
C'MON, I WANT YOU TWO TO REMEMBER THAT YOU WERE A PART OF THIS.
LAKERS 32
CHIPS
CANDY
BEER

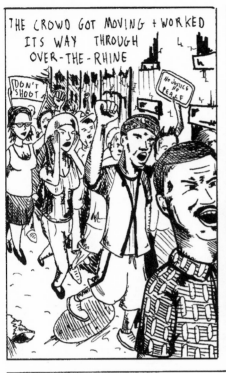

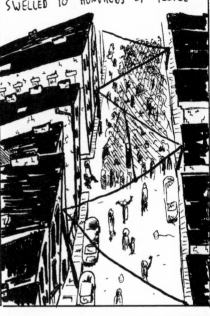

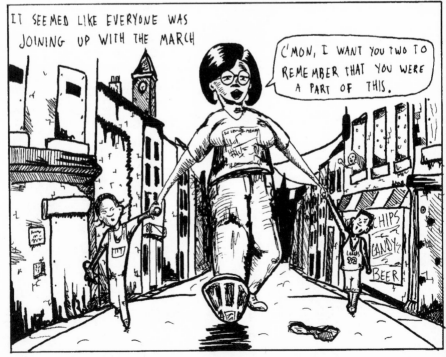

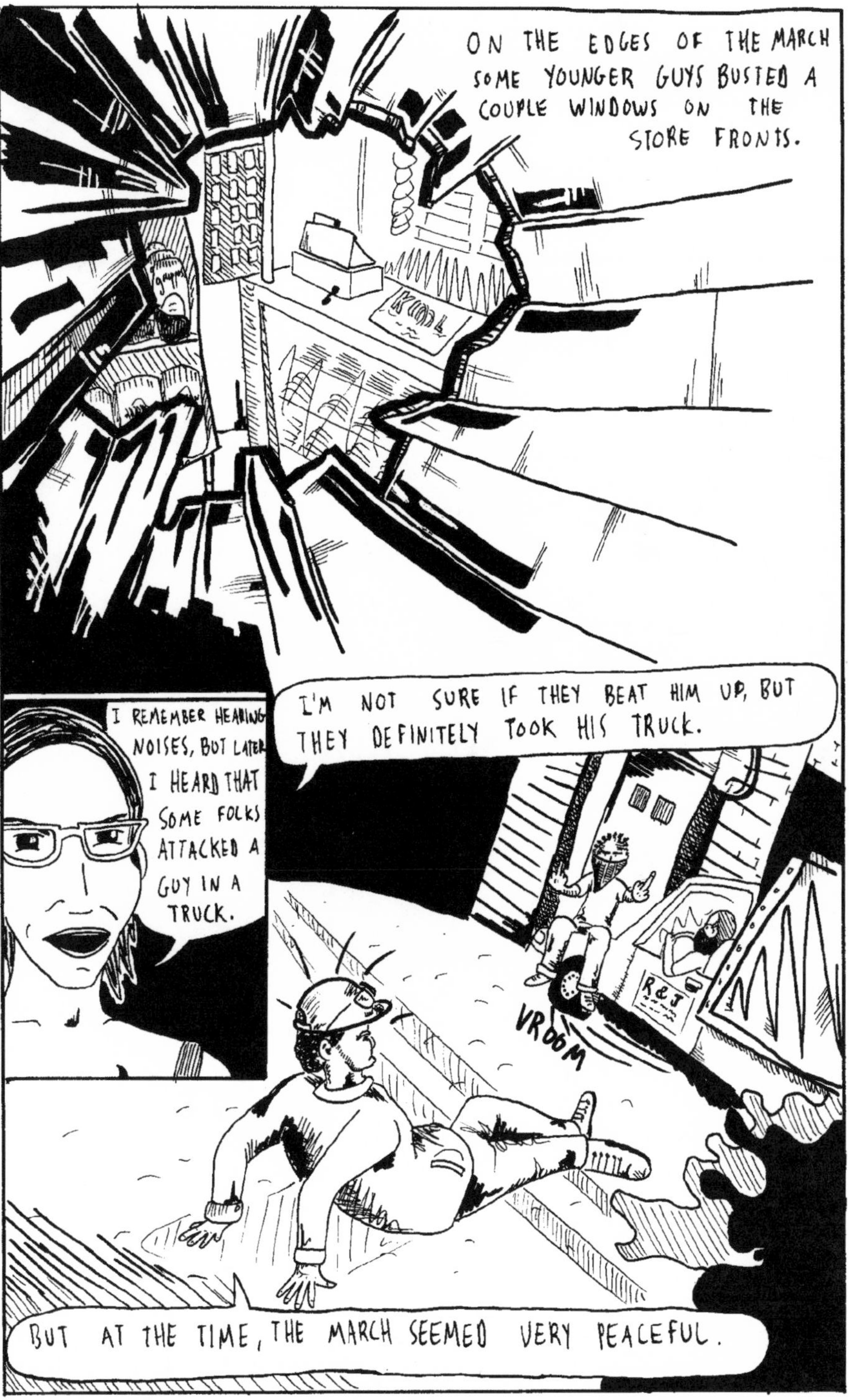

ON THE EDGES OF THE MARCH SOME YOUNGER GUYS BUSTED A COUPLE WINDOWS ON THE STORE FRONTS.
I REMEMBER HEARING NOISES, BUT LATER I HEARD THAT SOME FOLKS ATTACKED A GUY IN A TRUCK.
I'M NOT SURE IF THEY BEAT HIM UP, BUT THEY DEFINITELY TOOK HIS TRUCK.
R&J
VROOM
BUT AT THE TIME, THE MARCH SEEMED VERY PEACEFUL.

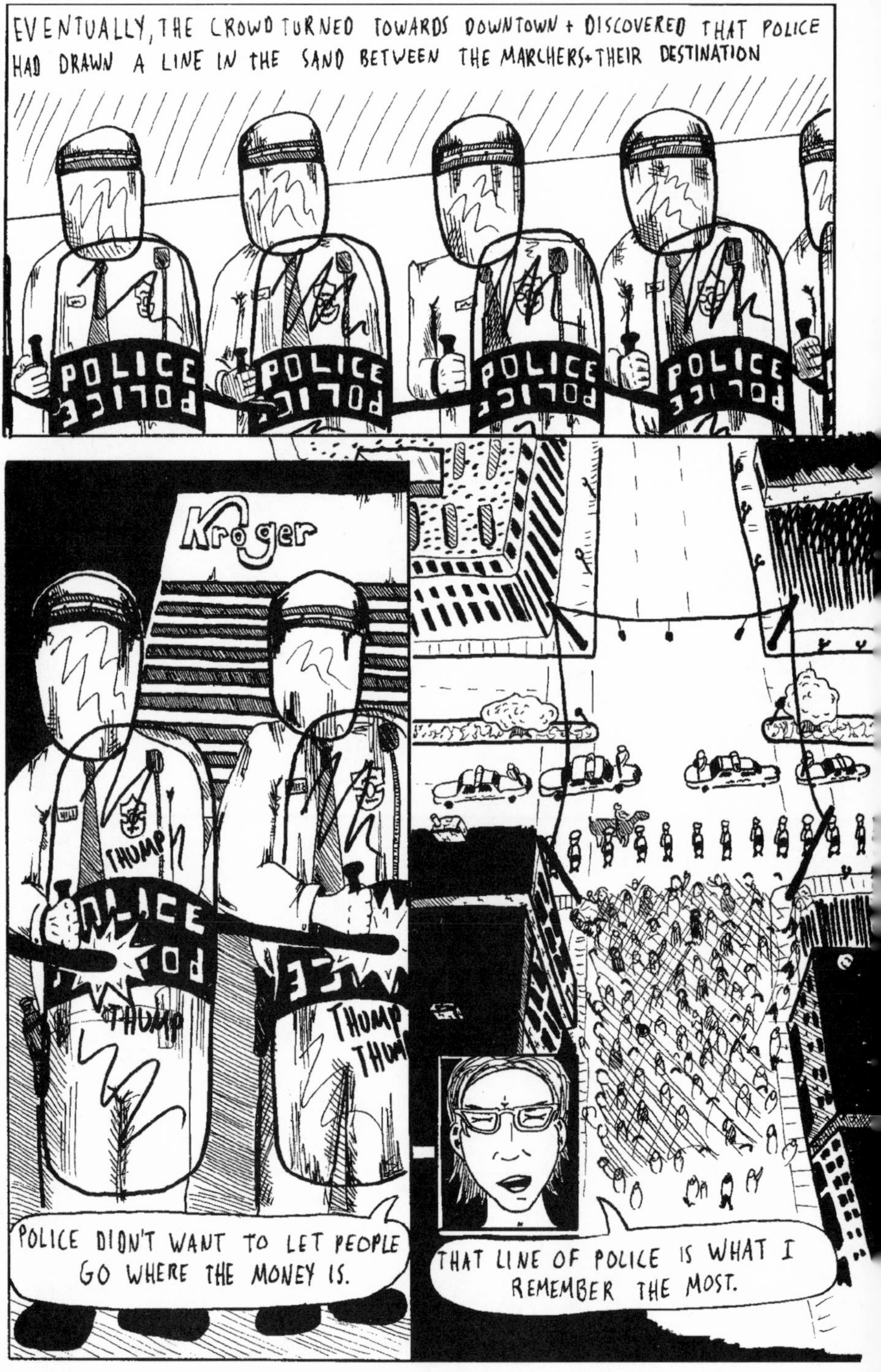
EVENTUALLY, THE CROWD TURNED TOWARDS DOWNTOWN + DISCOVERED THAT POLICE HAD DRAWN A LINE IN THE SAND BETWEEN THE MARCHERS+THEIR DESTINATION
POLICE
POLICE
POLICE
POLICE
POLICE
POLICE
POLICE
POLICE
Kroger
THUMP
THUMP
THUMP
THUM
POLICE DIDN'T WANT TO LET PEOPLE GO WHERE THE MONEY IS.
THAT LINE OF POLICE IS WHAT I REMEMBER THE MOST.

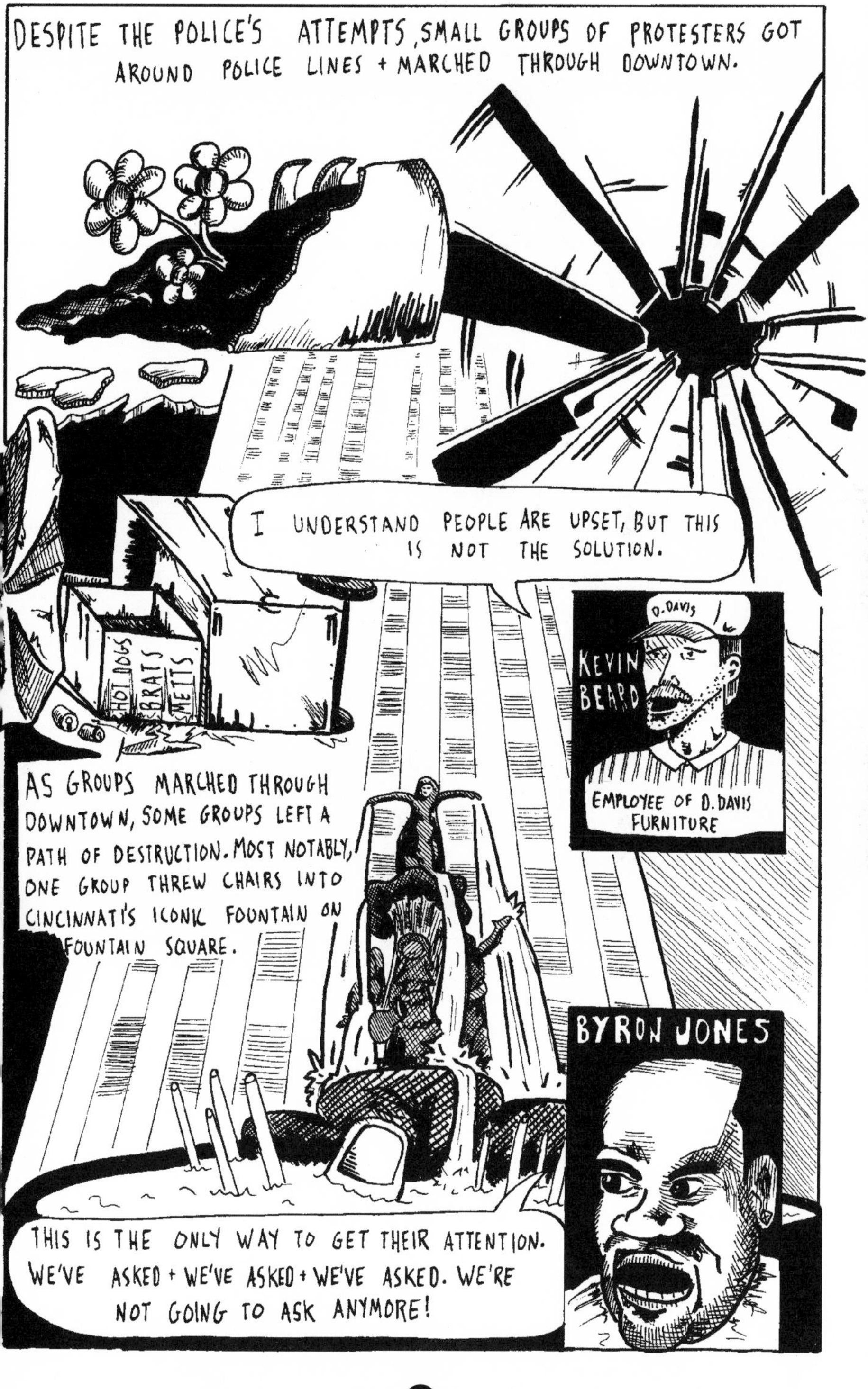

DESPITE THE POLICE'S ATTEMPTS, SMALL GROUPS OF PROTESTERS GOT AROUND POLICE LINES + MARCHED THROUGH DOWNTOWN.
I UNDERSTAND PEOPLE ARE UPSET, BUT THIS IS NOT THE SOLUTION.
D. DAVIS
KEVIN BEARD
EMPLOYEE OF D. DAVIS FURNITURE
HOT DOGS
BRATS
METTS
AS GROUPS MARCHED THROUGH DOWNTOWN, SOME GROUPS LEFT A PATH OF DESTRUCTION. MOST NOTABLY, ONE GROUP THREW CHAIRS INTO CINCINNATI'S ICONIC FOUNTAIN ON FOUNTAIN SQUARE.
BYRON JONES
THIS IS THE ONLY WAY TO GET THEIR ATTENTION. WE'VE ASKED + WE'VE ASKED + WE'VE ASKED. WE'RE NOT GOING TO ASK ANYMORE!

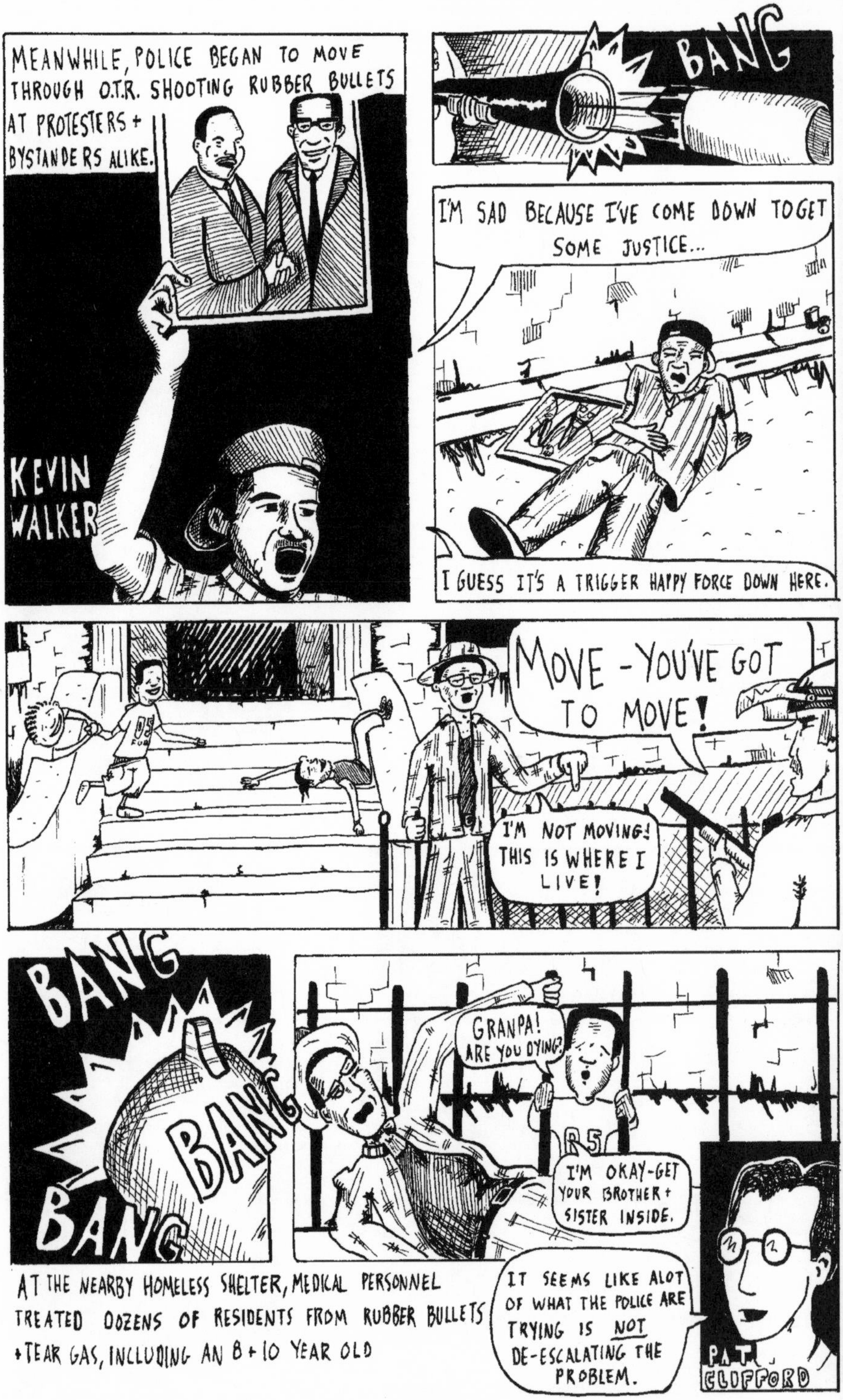
MEANWHILE, POLICE BEGAN TO MOVE THROUGH O.T.R. SHOOTING RUBBER BULLETS AT PROTESTERS + BYSTANDERS ALIKE.
KEVIN WALKER
BANG
I'M SAD BECAUSE I'VE COME DOWN TO GET SOME JUSTICE...
I GUESS IT'S A TRIGGER HAPPY FORCE DOWN HERE.
MOVE - YOU'VE GOT TO MOVE!
I'M NOT MOVING! THIS IS WHERE I LIVE!
BANG
BANG
BANG
GRANPA! ARE YOU DYING?
I'M OKAY-GET YOUR BROTHER + SISTER INSIDE.
AT THE NEARBY HOMELESS SHELTER, MEDICAL PERSONNEL TREATED DOZENS OF RESIDENTS FROM RUBBER BULLETS + TEAR GAS, INCLUDING AN 8 + 10 YEAR OLD
IT SEEMS LIKE ALOT OF WHAT THE POLICE ARE TRYING IS NOT DE-ESCALATING THE PROBLEM.
PAT CLIFFORD

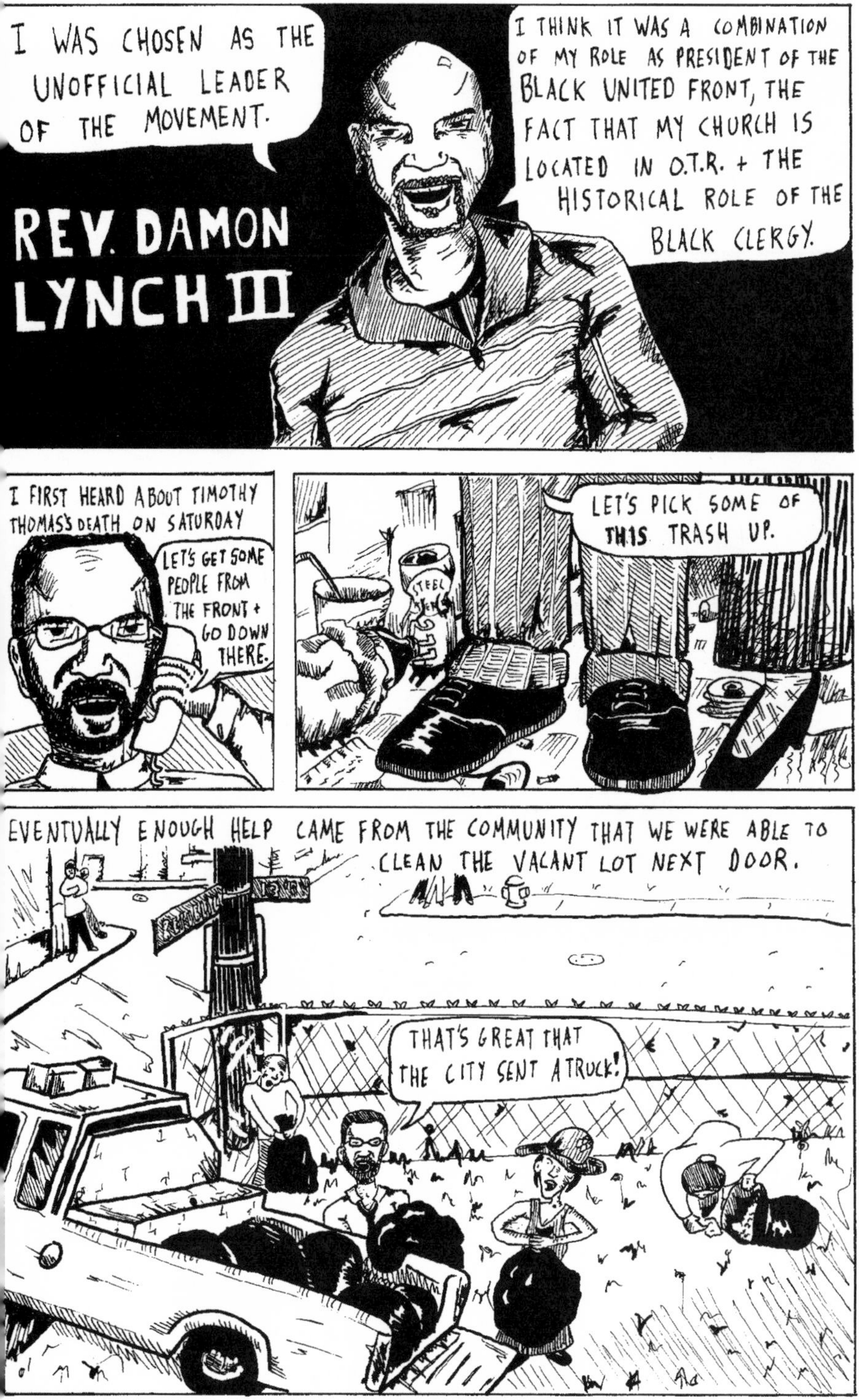

I WAS CHOSEN AS THE UNOFFICIAL LEADER OF THE MOVEMENT.
I THINK IT WAS A COMBINATION OF MY ROLE AS PRESIDENT OF THE BLACK UNITED FRONT, THE FACT THAT MY CHURCH IS LOCATED IN O.T.R. + THE HISTORICAL ROLE OF THE BLACK CLERGY.
REV. DAMON LYNCH III
I FIRST HEARD ABOUT TIMOTHY THOMAS'S DEATH ON SATURDAY
LET'S GET SOME PEOPLE FROM THE FRONT + GO DOWN THERE.
LET'S PICK SOME OF THIS TRASH UP.
EVENTUALLY ENOUGH HELP CAME FROM THE COMMUNITY THAT WE WERE ABLE TO CLEAN THE VACANT LOT NEXT DOOR.
THAT'S GREAT THAT THE CITY SENT A TRUCK!

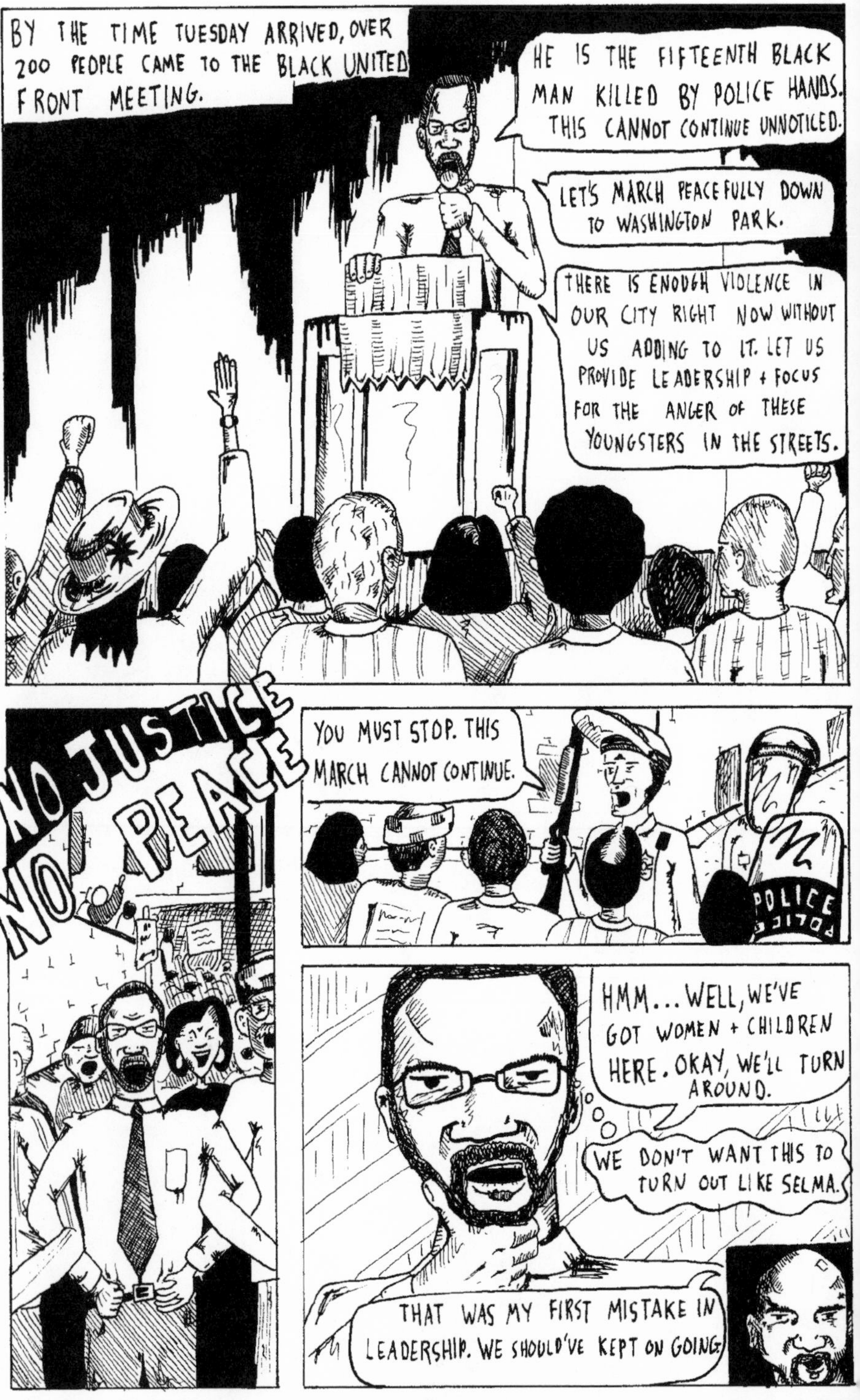
BY THE TIME TUESDAY ARRIVED, OVER 200 PEOPLE CAME TO THE BLACK UNITED FRONT MEETING.
HE IS THE FIFTEENTH BLACK MAN KILLED BY POLICE HANDS. THIS CANNOT CONTINUE UNNOTICED.
LET'S MARCH PEACEFULLY DOWN TO WASHINGTON PARK.
THERE IS ENOUGH VIOLENCE IN OUR CITY RIGHT NOW WITHOUT US ADDING TO IT. LET US PROVIDE LEADERSHIP + FOCUS FOR THE ANGER OF THESE YOUNGSTERS IN THE STREETS.
NO JUSTICE NO PEACE
YOU MUST STOP. THIS MARCH CANNOT CONTINUE.
POLICE
HMM... WELL, WE'VE GOT WOMEN + CHILDREN HERE. OKAY, WE'LL TURN AROUND.
WE DON'T WANT THIS TO TURN OUT LIKE SELMA.
THAT WAS MY FIRST MISTAKE IN LEADERSHIP. WE SHOULD'VE KEPT ON GOING.

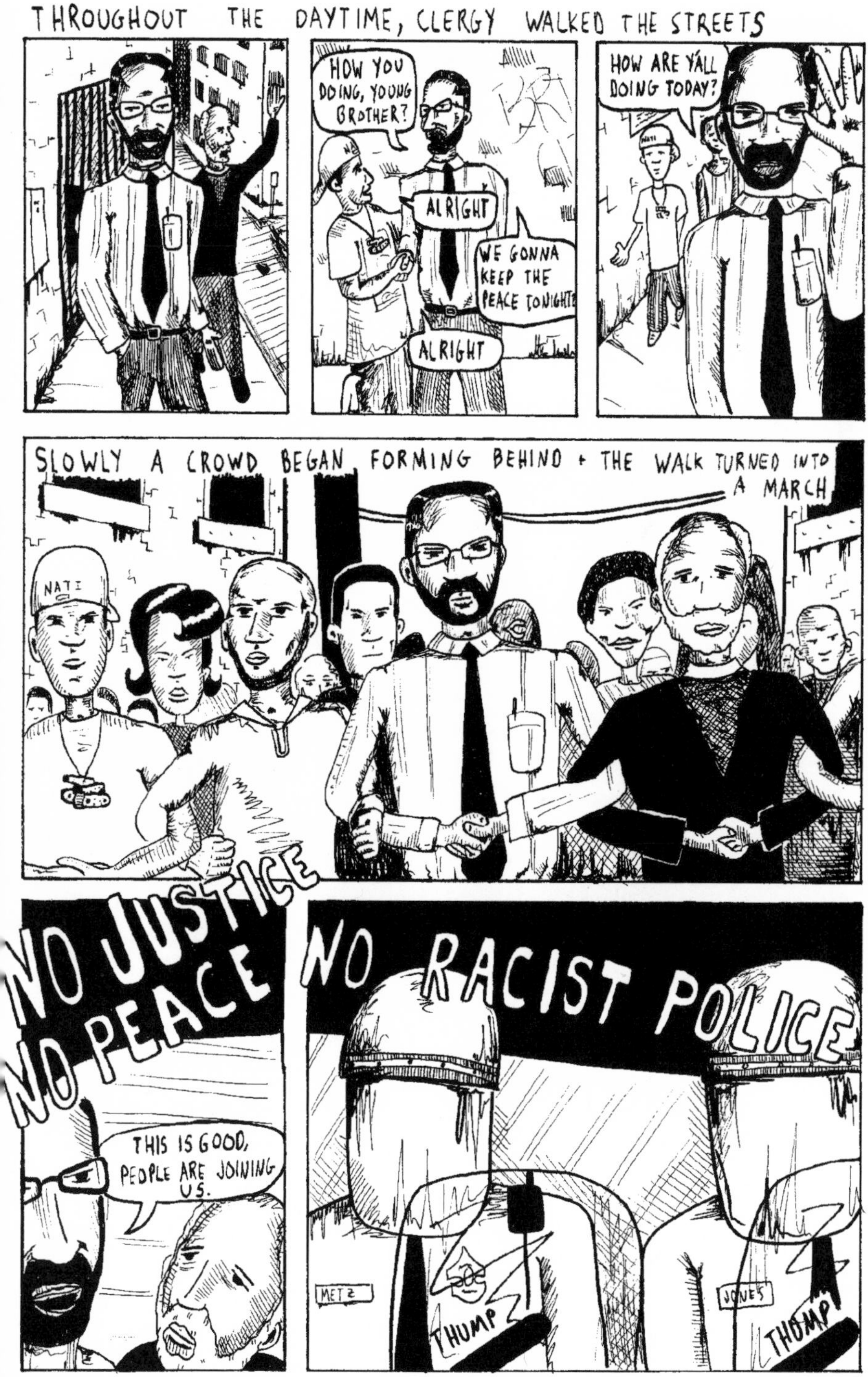
THROUGHOUT THE DAYTIME, CLERGY WALKED THE STREETS
HOW YOU DOING, YOUNG BROTHER?
ALRIGHT
WE GONNA KEEP THE PEACE TONIGHT?
ALRIGHT
HOW ARE Y'ALL DOING TODAY?
SLOWLY A CROWD BEGAN FORMING BEHIND + THE WALK TURNED INTO A MARCH
NATI
NO JUSTICE NO PEACE
THIS IS GOOD, PEOPLE ARE JOINING US.
NO RACIST POLICE
METZ
THUMP
JONES
THUMP

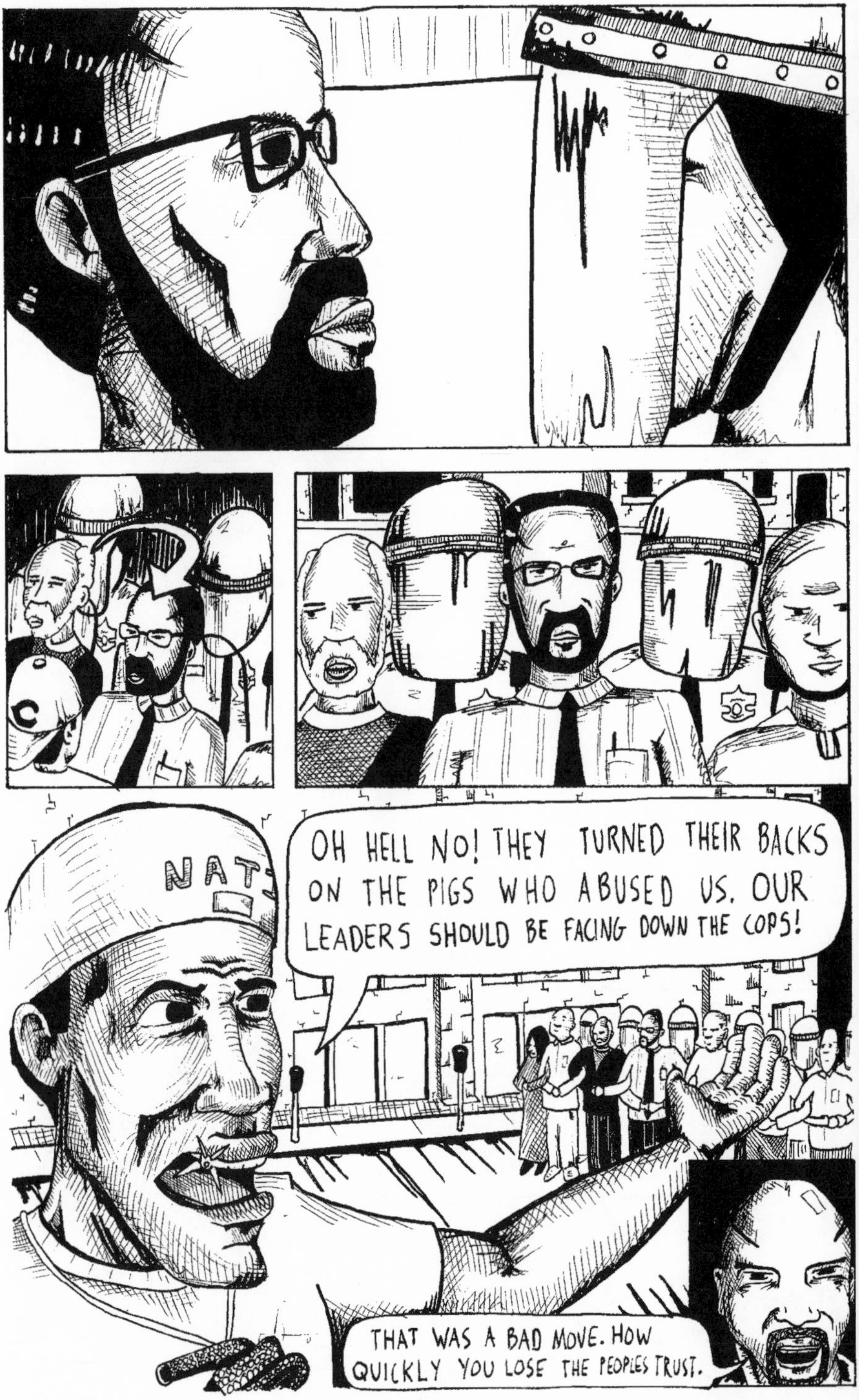
NAT
OH HELL NO! THEY TURNED THEIR BACKS ON THE PIGS WHO ABUSED US. OUR LEADERS SHOULD BE FACING DOWN THE COPS!
THAT WAS A BAD MOVE. HOW QUICKLY YOU LOSE THE PEOPLES TRUST.

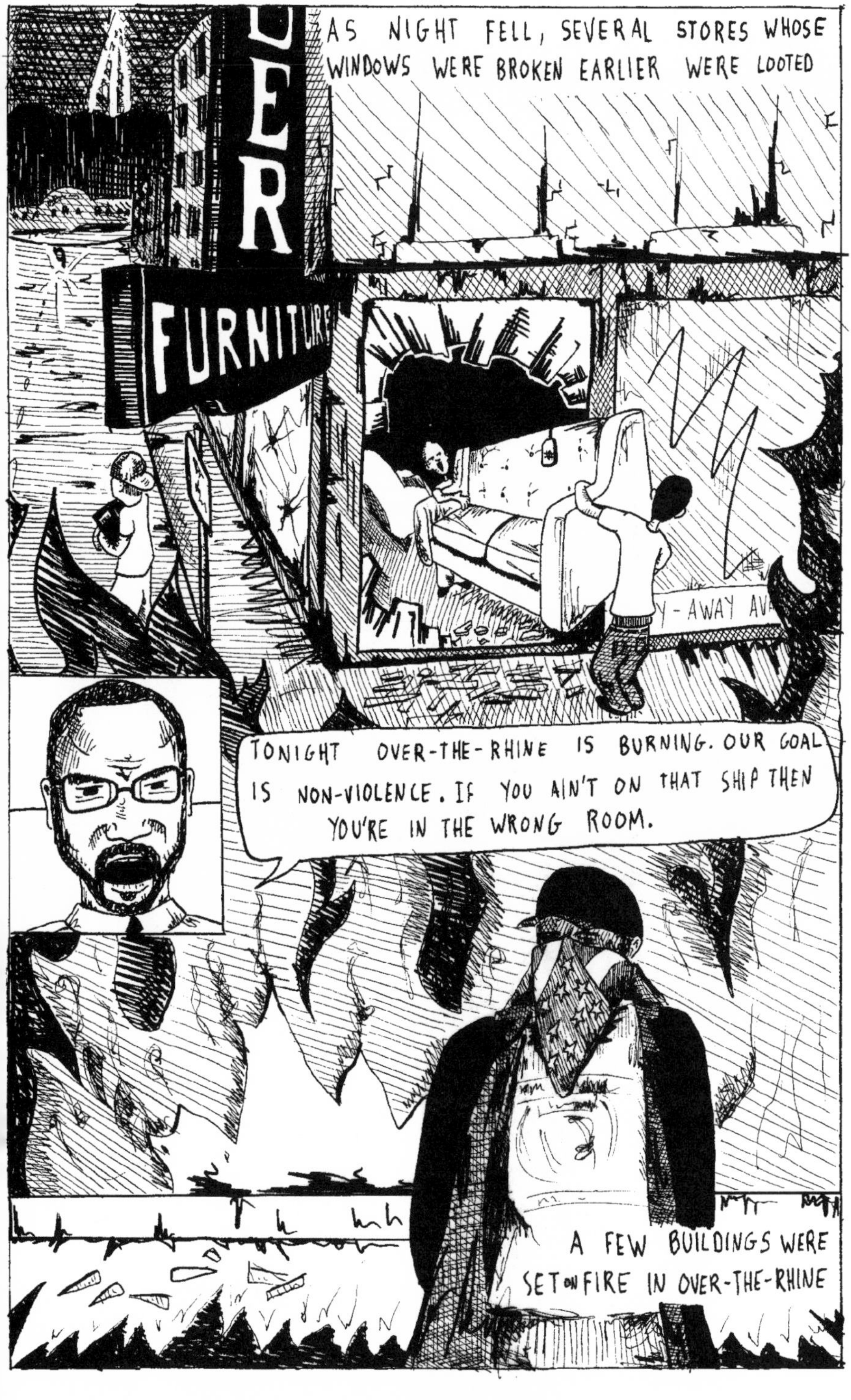
AS NIGHT FELL, SEVERAL STORES WHOSE WINDOWS WERE BROKEN EARLIER WERE LOOTED
FURNITURE
Y-AWAY AV
TONIGHT OVER-THE-RHINE IS BURNING. OUR GOAL IS NON-VIOLENCE. IF YOU AIN'T ON THAT SHIP THEN YOU'RE IN THE WRONG ROOM.
A FEW BUILDINGS WERE SET ON FIRE IN OVER-THE-RHINE

WEDNESDAY

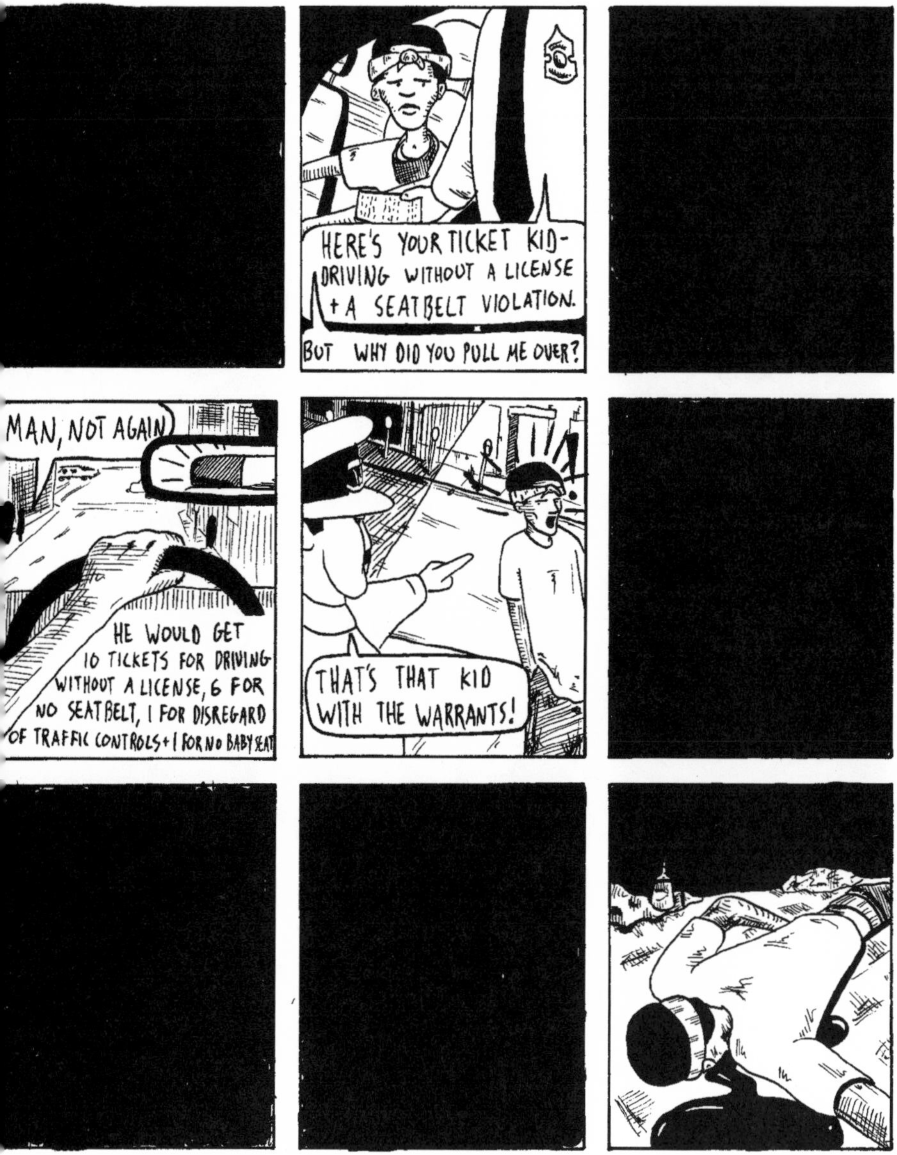
HERE'S YOUR TICKET KID- DRIVING WITHOUT A LICENSE + A SEATBELT VIOLATION.
BUT WHY DID YOU PULL ME OVER?
MAN, NOT AGAIN
HE WOULD GET 10 TICKETS FOR DRIVING WITHOUT A LICENSE, 6 FOR NO SEATBELT, 1 FOR DISREGARD OF TRAFFIC CONTROLS + 1 FOR NO BABY SEAT
THAT'S THAT KID WITH THE WARRANTS!

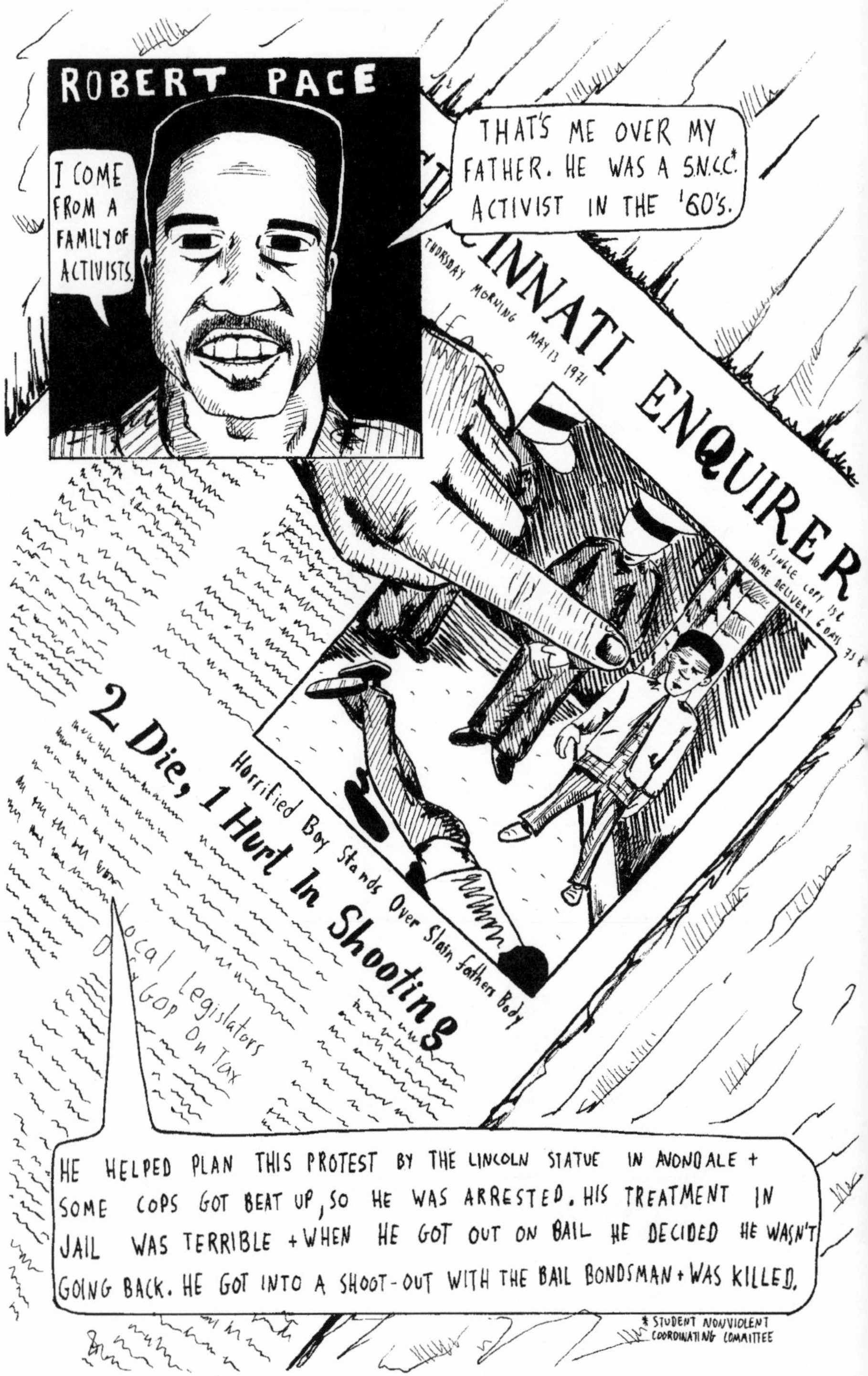
ROBERT PACE
I COME FROM A FAMILY OF ACTIVISTS.
THAT'S ME OVER MY FATHER. HE WAS A S.N.C.C.* ACTIVIST IN THE '60's.
INNATI ENQUIRER
THURSDAY MORNING MAY 13 1971
SINGLE COPY 15¢
2 Die, 1 Hurt In Shooting
Horrified Boy Stands Over Slain Fathers Body
Local Legislators On Tax
HE HELPED PLAN THIS PROTEST BY THE LINCOLN STATUE IN AVONDALE + SOME COPS GOT BEAT UP, SO HE WAS ARRESTED. HIS TREATMENT IN JAIL WAS TERRIBLE + WHEN HE GOT OUT ON BAIL HE DECIDED HE WASN'T GOING BACK. HE GOT INTO A SHOOT-OUT WITH THE BAIL BONDSMAN + WAS KILLED.
* STUDENT NONVIOLENT COORDINATING COMMITTEE

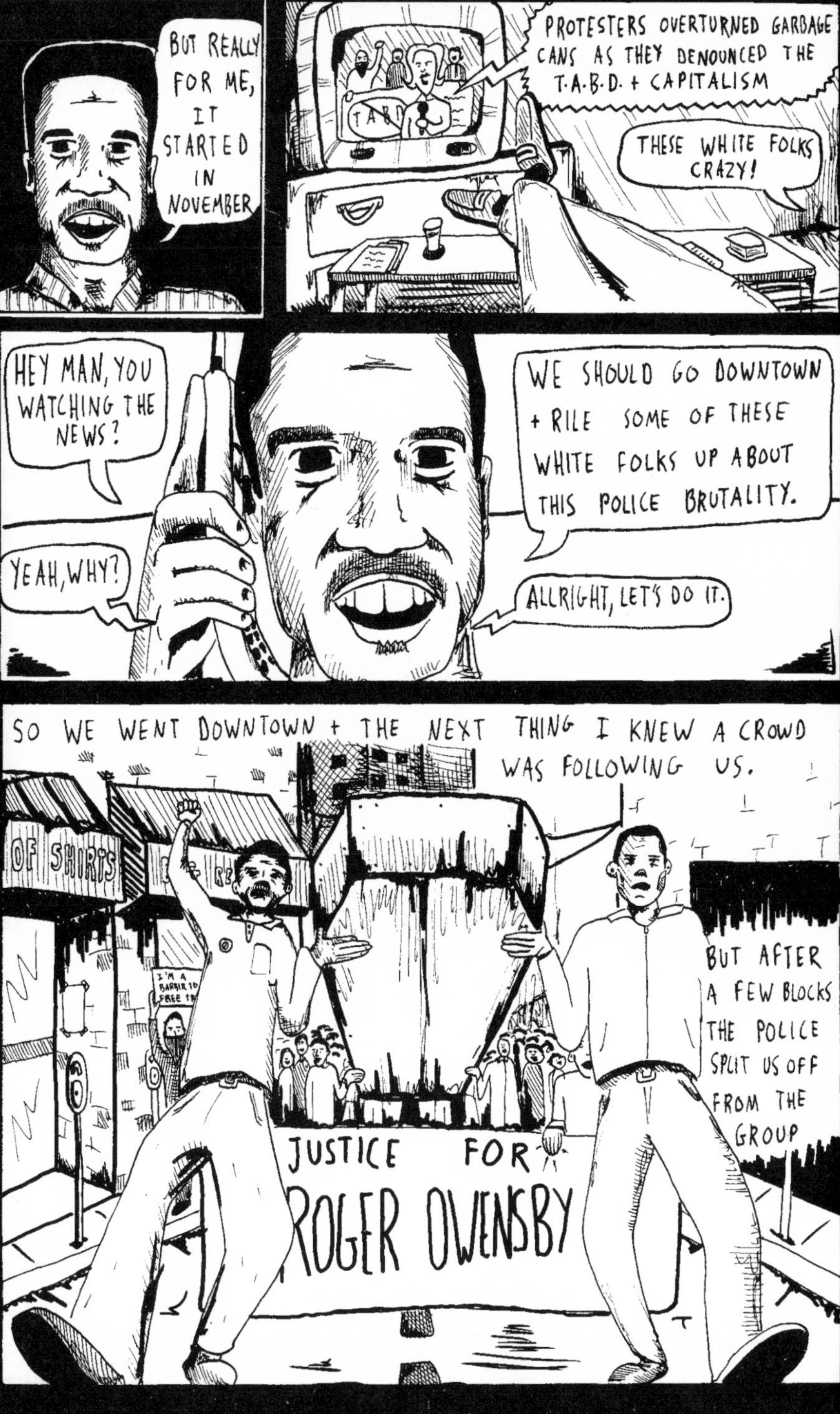
BUT REALLY FOR ME, IT STARTED IN NOVEMBER
PROTESTERS OVERTURNED GARBAGE CANS AS THEY DENOUNCED THE T.A.B.D. + CAPITALISM
THESE WHITE FOLKS CRAZY!
HEY MAN, YOU WATCHING THE NEWS?
YEAH, WHY?
WE SHOULD GO DOWNTOWN + RILE SOME OF THESE WHITE FOLKS UP ABOUT THIS POLICE BRUTALITY.
ALLRIGHT, LET'S DO IT.
SO WE WENT DOWNTOWN + THE NEXT THING I KNEW A CROWD WAS FOLLOWING US.
OF SHIRTS
JUSTICE FOR ROGER OWENSBY
BUT AFTER A FEW BLOCKS THE POLICE SPLIT US OFF FROM THE GROUP

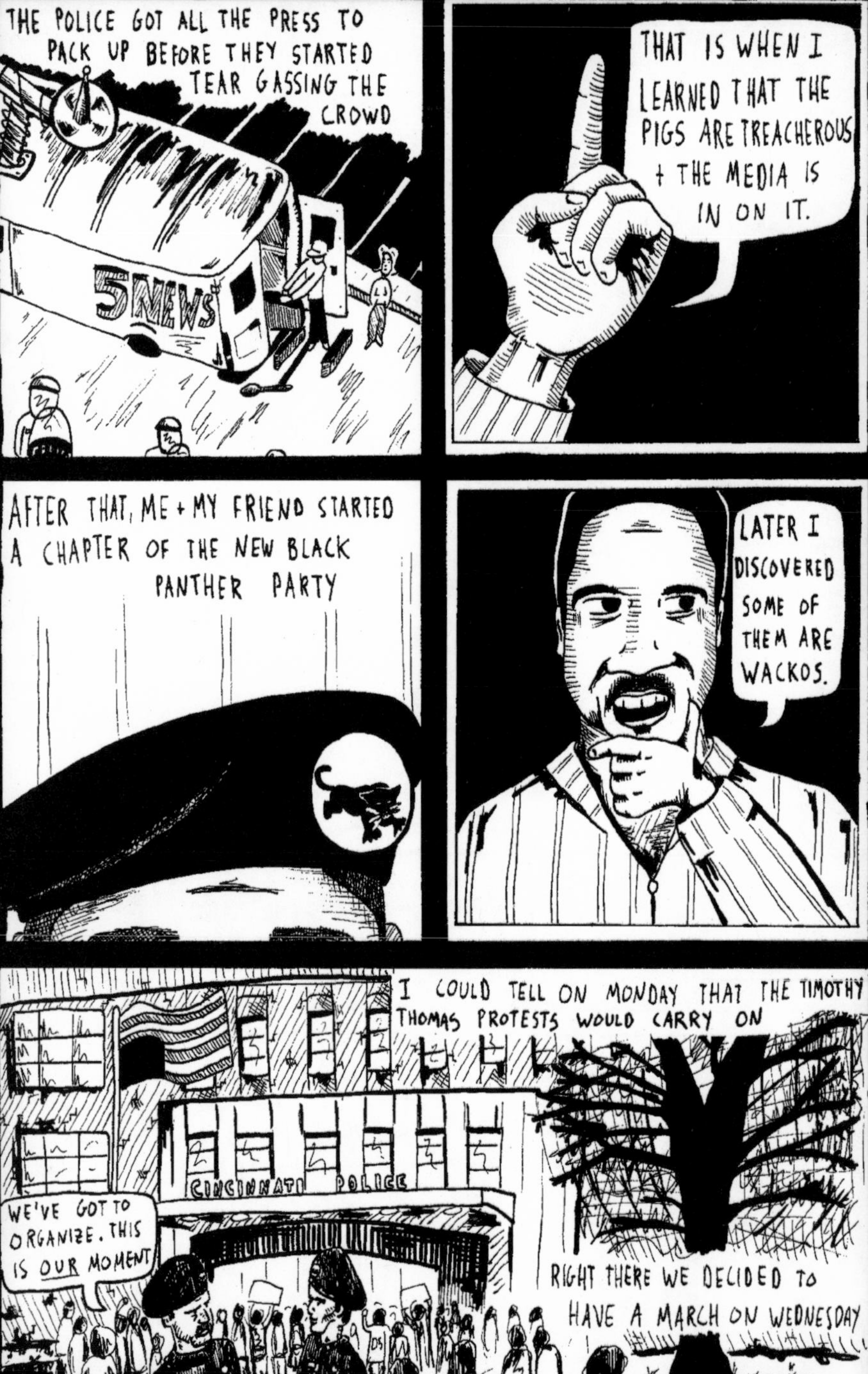
THE POLICE GOT ALL THE PRESS TO PACK UP BEFORE THEY STARTED TEAR GASSING THE CROWD
5 NEWS
THAT IS WHEN I LEARNED THAT THE PIGS ARE TREACHEROUS + THE MEDIA IS IN ON IT.
AFTER THAT, ME + MY FRIEND STARTED A CHAPTER OF THE NEW BLACK PANTHER PARTY
LATER I DISCOVERED SOME OF THEM ARE WACKOS.
I COULD TELL ON MONDAY THAT THE TIMOTHY THOMAS PROTESTS WOULD CARRY ON
CINCINNATI POLICE
WE'VE GOT TO ORGANIZE. THIS IS OUR MOMENT
RIGHT THERE WE DECIDED TO HAVE A MARCH ON WEDNESDAY

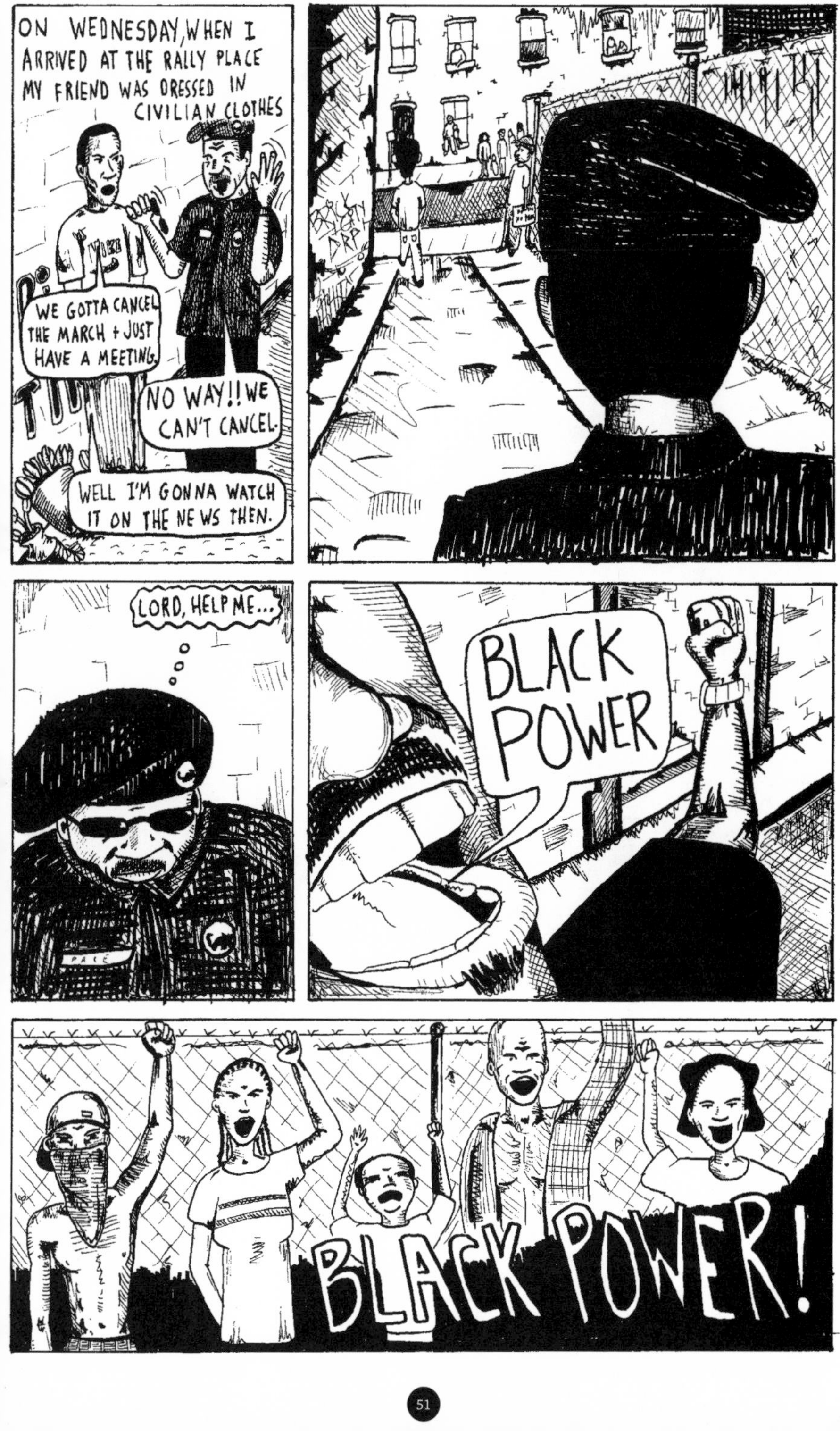
ON WEDNESDAY, WHEN I ARRIVED AT THE RALLY PLACE MY FRIEND WAS DRESSED IN CIVILIAN CLOTHES
WE GOTTA CANCEL THE MARCH + JUST HAVE A MEETING.
NO WAY!! WE CAN'T CANCEL.
WELL I'M GONNA WATCH IT ON THE NEWS THEN.
LORD, HELP ME...
BLACK POWER
BLACK POWER!

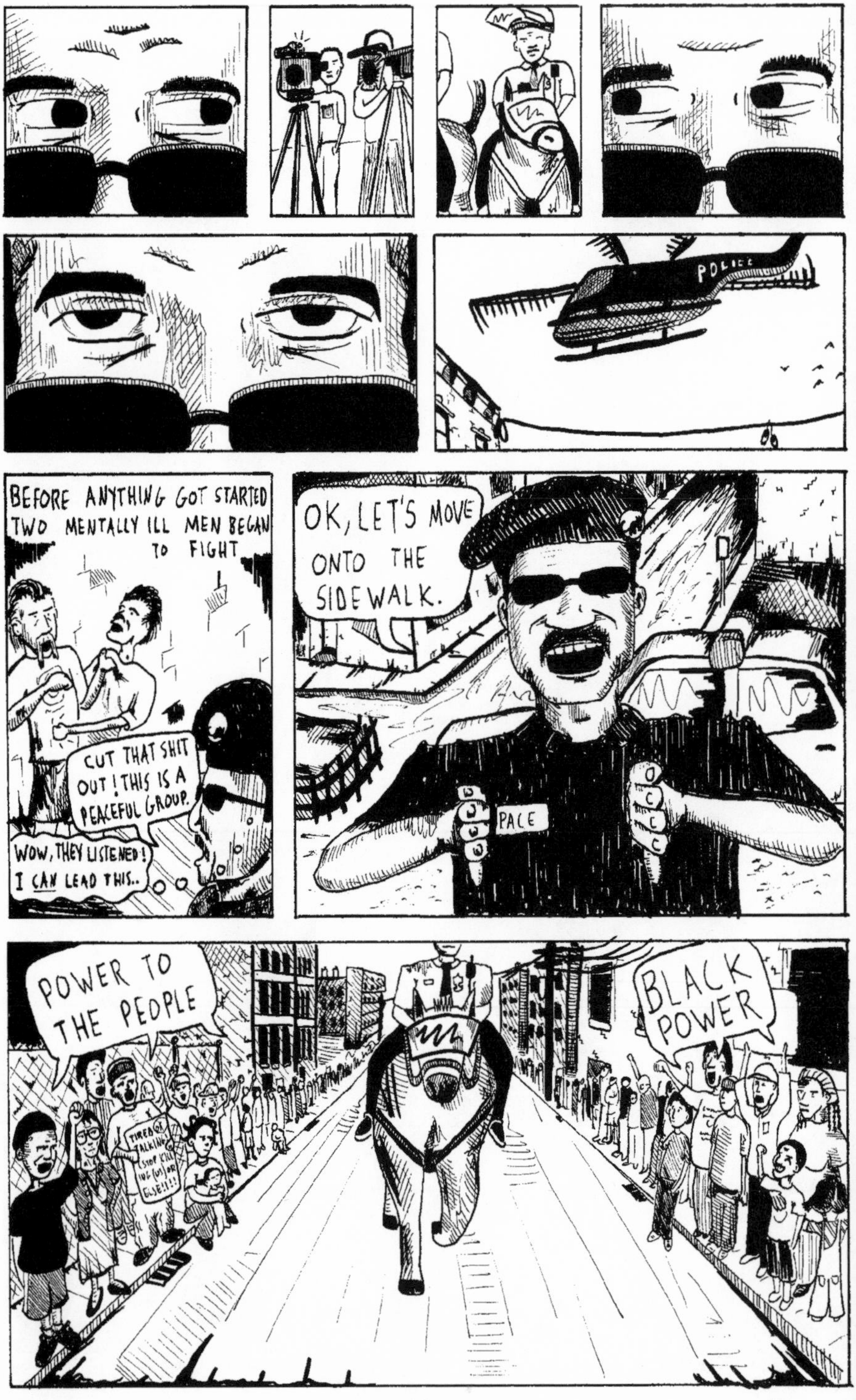

POLICE
BEFORE ANYTHING GOT STARTED TWO MENTALLY ILL MEN BEGAN TO FIGHT
CUT THAT SHIT OUT! THIS IS A PEACEFUL GROUP.
WOW, THEY LISTENED! I CAN LEAD THIS..
OK, LET'S MOVE ONTO THE SIDEWALK.
PACE
POWER TO THE PEOPLE
BLACK POWER

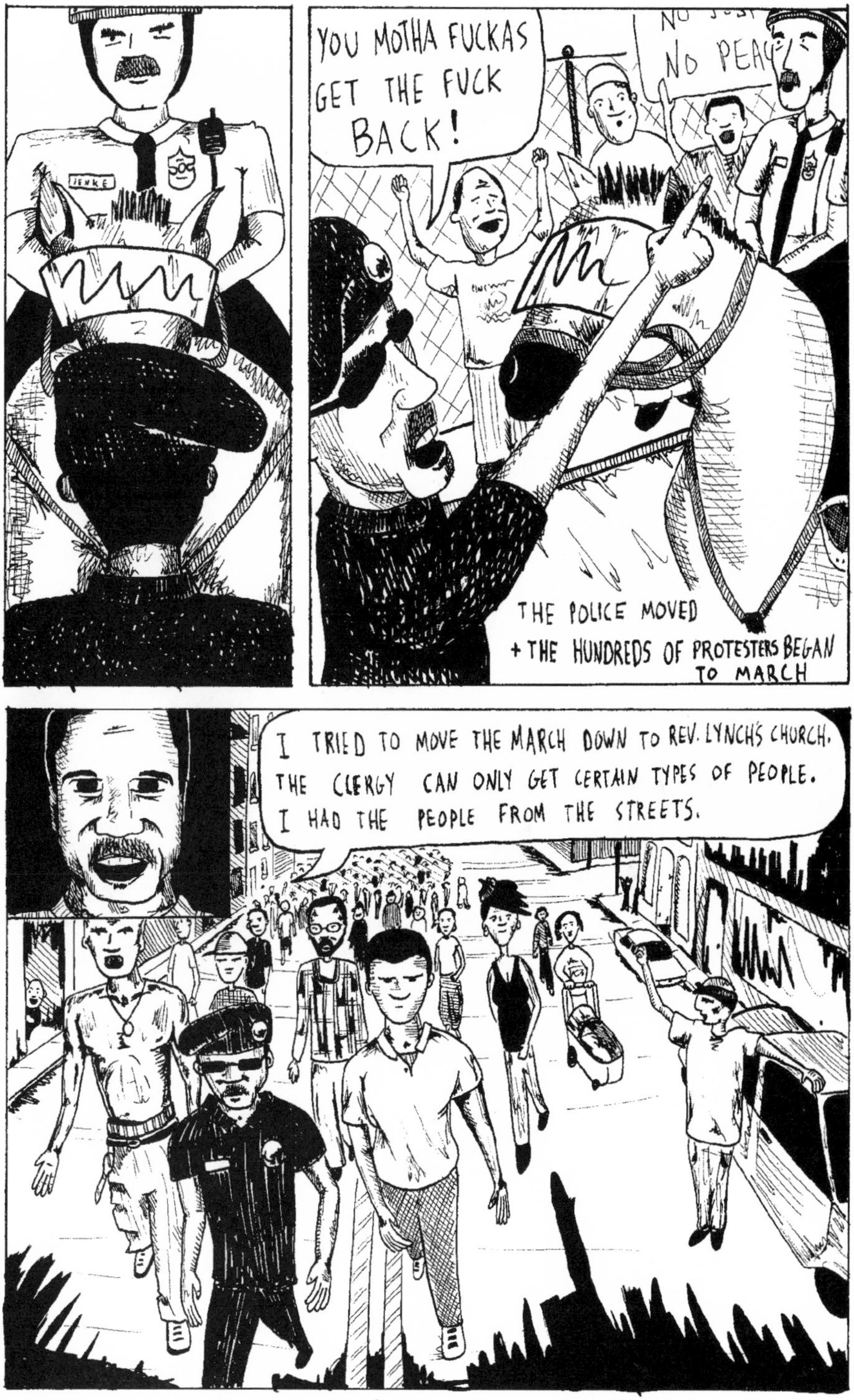
JENKE
YOU MOTHA FUCKAS GET THE FUCK BACK!
THE POLICE MOVED + THE HUNDREDS OF PROTESTERS BEGAN TO MARCH
I TRIED TO MOVE THE MARCH DOWN TO REV. LYNCH'S CHURCH. THE CLERGY CAN ONLY GET CERTAIN TYPES OF PEOPLE. I HAD THE PEOPLE FROM THE STREETS.

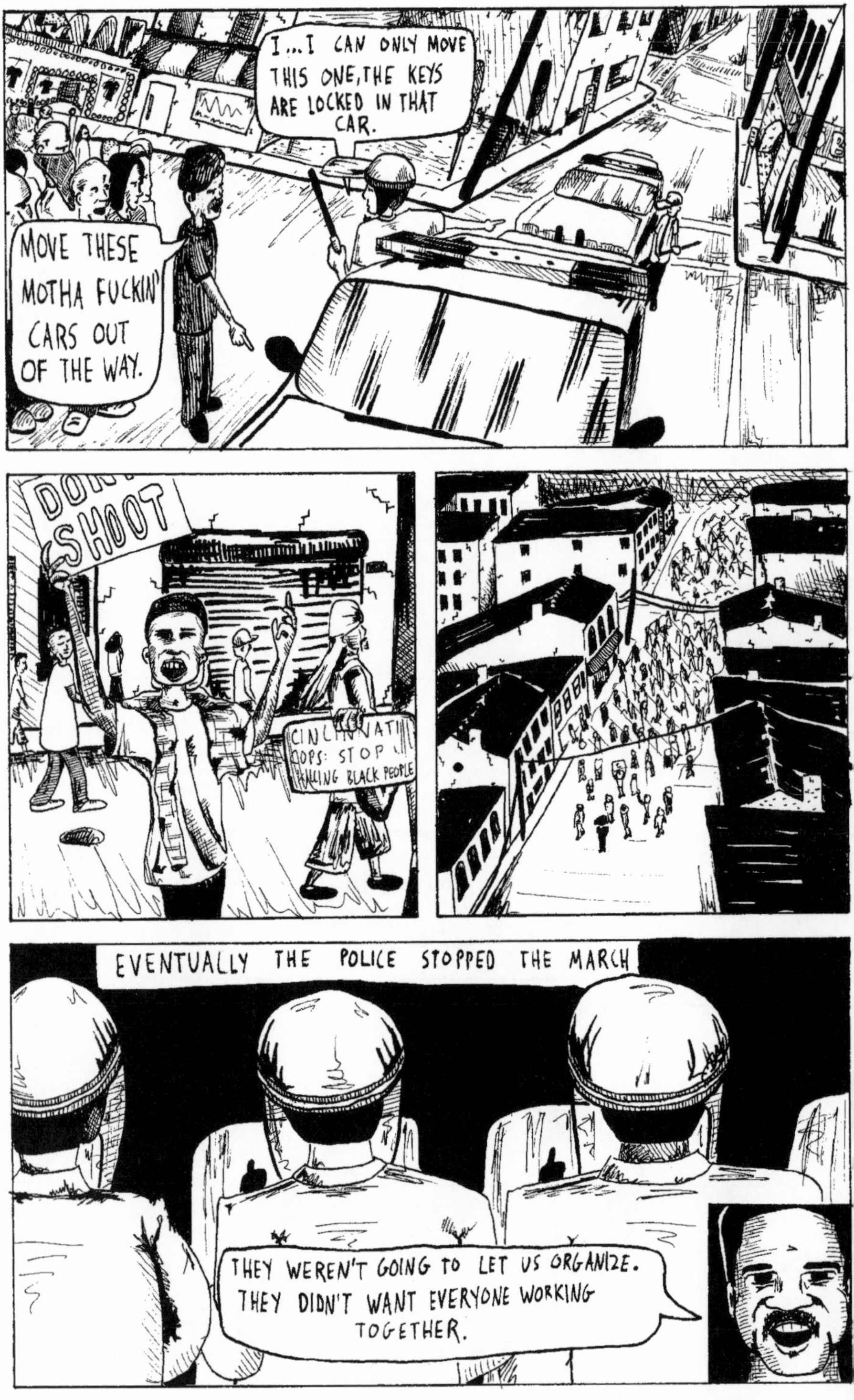
I...I CAN ONLY MOVE THIS ONE, THE KEYS ARE LOCKED IN THAT CAR.
MOVE THESE MOTHA FUCKIN' CARS OUT OF THE WAY.
SHOOT
CINCINNATI COPS: STOP KILLING BLACK PEOPLE
EVENTUALLY THE POLICE STOPPED THE MARCH
THEY WEREN'T GOING TO LET US ORGANIZE. THEY DIDN'T WANT EVERYONE WORKING TOGETHER.

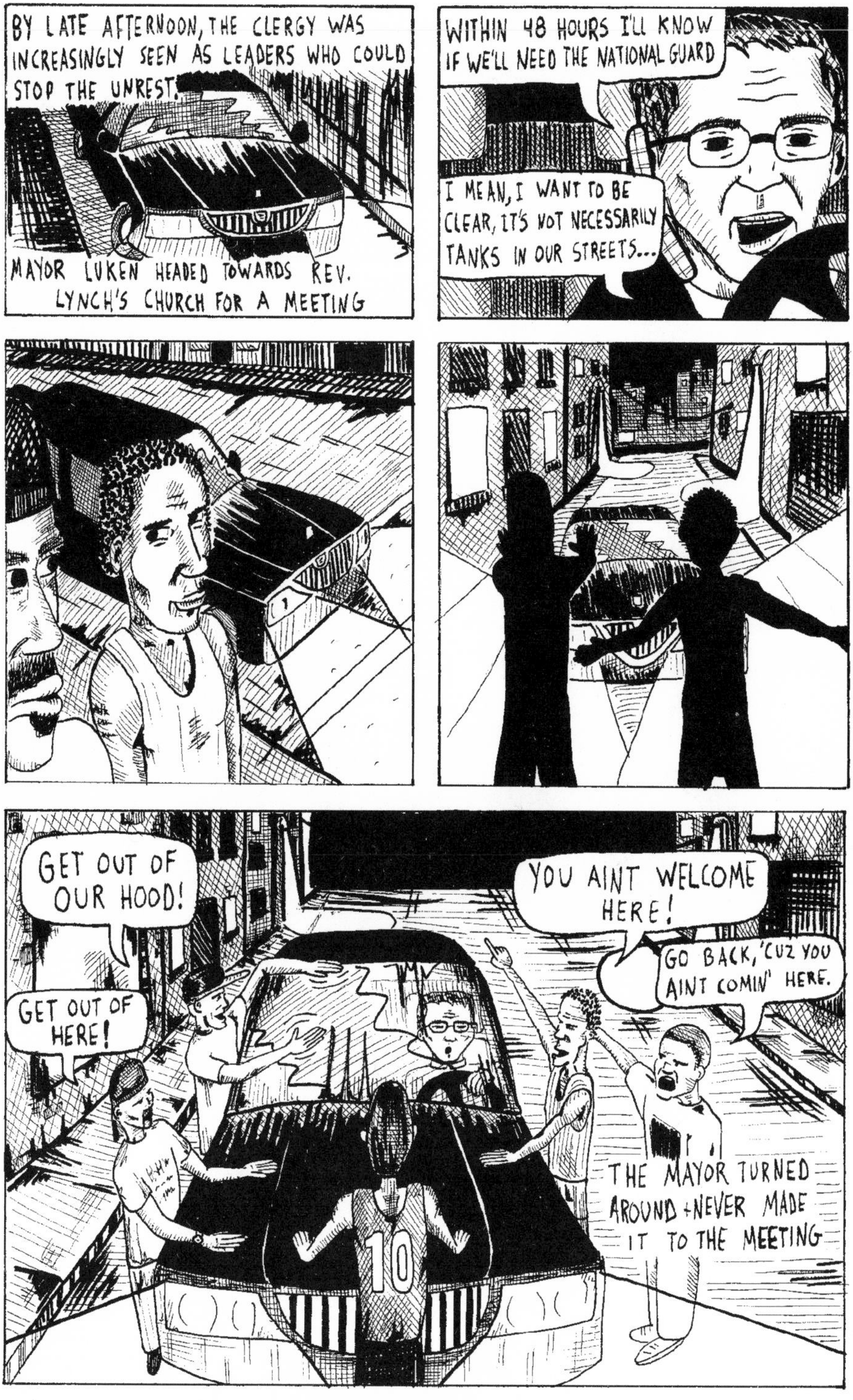
BY LATE AFTERNOON, THE CLERGY WAS INCREASINGLY SEEN AS LEADERS WHO COULD STOP THE UNREST.
MAYOR LUKEN HEADED TOWARDS REV. LYNCH'S CHURCH FOR A MEETING
WITHIN 48 HOURS I'LL KNOW IF WE'LL NEED THE NATIONAL GUARD
I MEAN, I WANT TO BE CLEAR, IT'S NOT NECESSARILY TANKS IN OUR STREETS...
GET OUT OF OUR HOOD!
YOU AINT WELCOME HERE!
GO BACK, 'CUZ YOU AINT COMIN' HERE.
GET OUT OF HERE!
THE MAYOR TURNED AROUND + NEVER MADE IT TO THE MEETING
10

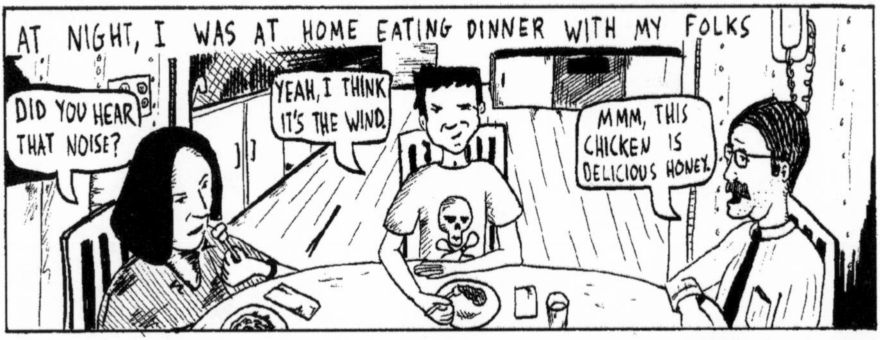
AT NIGHT, I WAS AT HOME EATING DINNER WITH MY FOLKS
DID YOU HEAR THAT NOISE?
YEAH, I THINK IT'S THE WIND.
MMM, THIS CHICKEN IS DELICIOUS HONEY.

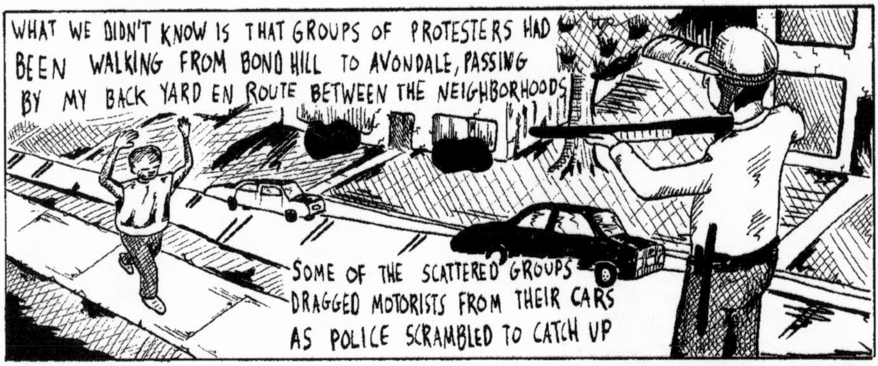
WHAT WE DIDN'T KNOW IS THAT GROUPS OF PROTESTERS HAD BEEN WALKING FROM BOND HILL TO AVONDALE, PASSING BY MY BACK YARD EN ROUTE BETWEEN THE NEIGHBORHOODS
SOME OF THE SCATTERED GROUPS DRAGGED MOTORISTS FROM THEIR CARS AS POLICE SCRAMBLED TO CATCH UP

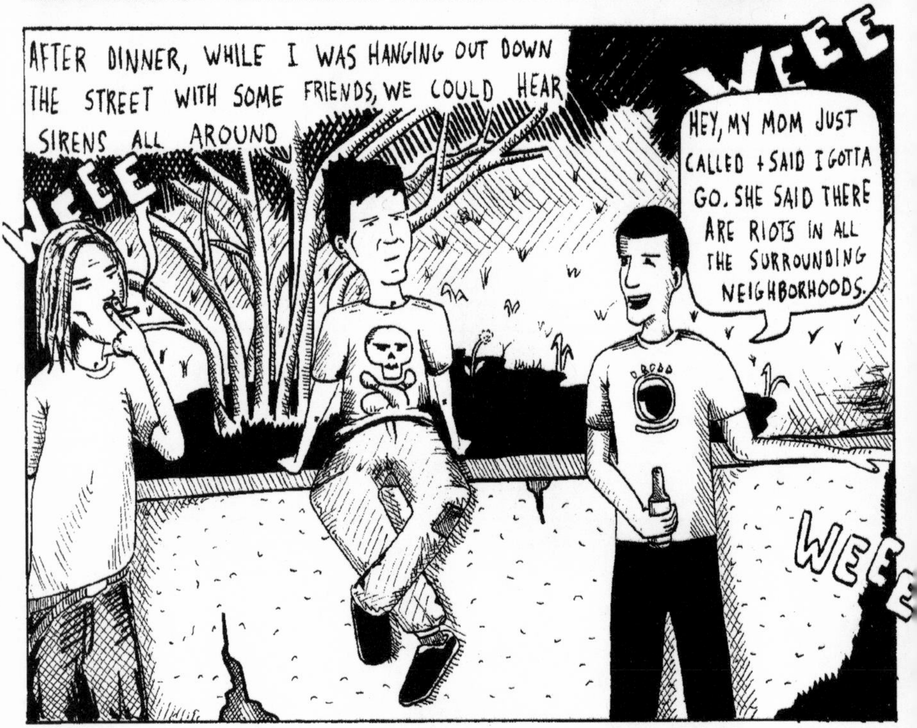
AFTER DINNER, WHILE I WAS HANGING OUT DOWN THE STREET WITH SOME FRIENDS, WE COULD HEAR SIRENS ALL AROUND
WEEE
WEEE
HEY, MY MOM JUST CALLED + SAID I GOTTA GO. SHE SAID THERE ARE RIOTS IN ALL THE SURROUNDING NEIGHBORHOODS.
WEEE

IT WAS TRUE. PROPERTY DAMAGE, WHICH HAD BEEN CONFINED TO OVER-THE-RHINE THE PRIOR NIGHT, HAD SPREAD TO SEVERAL PREDOMINENTLY BLACK COMMUNITIES

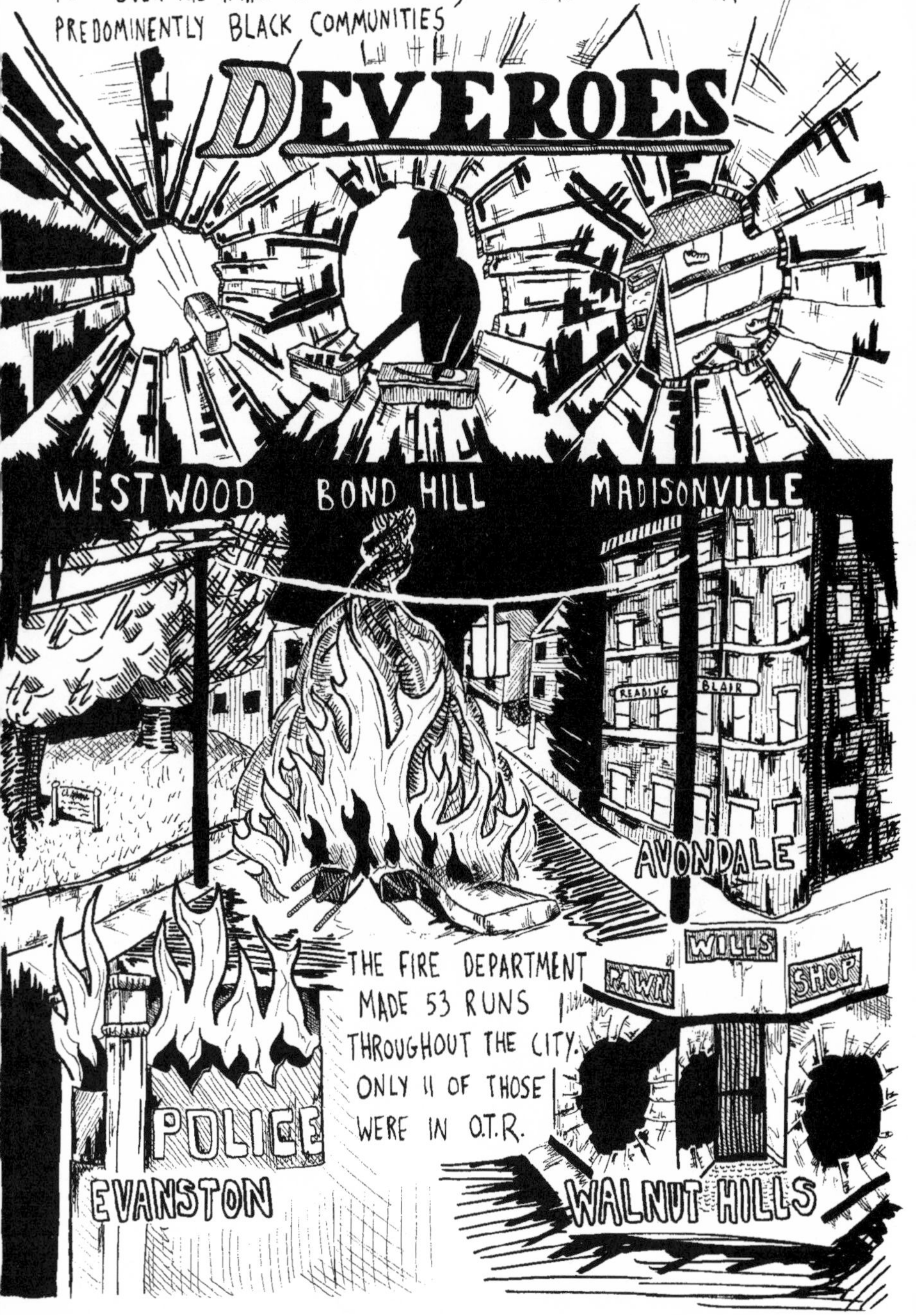

DEVEROES
WESTWOOD
BOND HILL
MADISONVILLE
READING
BLAIR
AVONDALE
WILLS
PAWN
SHOP
THE FIRE DEPARTMENT MADE 53 RUNS THROUGHOUT THE CITY. ONLY 11 OF THOSE WERE IN O.T.R.
POLICE
EVANSTON
WALNUT HILLS

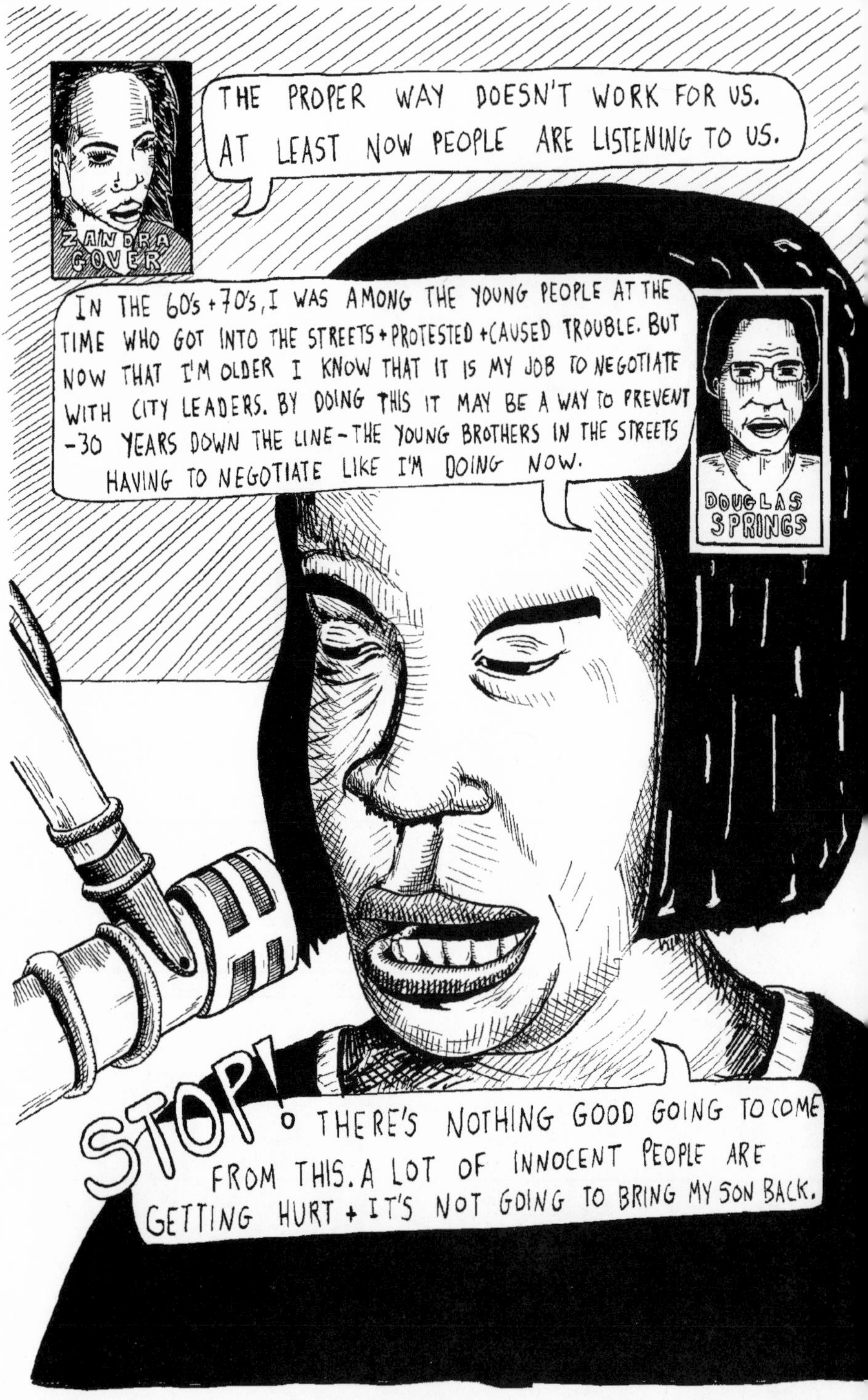
ZANDRA GOVER
THE PROPER WAY DOESN'T WORK FOR US. AT LEAST NOW PEOPLE ARE LISTENING TO US.
IN THE 60's + 70's, I WAS AMONG THE YOUNG PEOPLE AT THE TIME WHO GOT INTO THE STREETS + PROTESTED + CAUSED TROUBLE. BUT NOW THAT I'M OLDER I KNOW THAT IT IS MY JOB TO NEGOTIATE WITH CITY LEADERS. BY DOING THIS IT MAY BE A WAY TO PREVENT -30 YEARS DOWN THE LINE- THE YOUNG BROTHERS IN THE STREETS HAVING TO NEGOTIATE LIKE I'M DOING NOW.
DOUGLAS SPRINGS
STOP! THERE'S NOTHING GOOD GOING TO COME FROM THIS. A LOT OF INNOCENT PEOPLE ARE GETTING HURT + IT'S NOT GOING TO BRING MY SON BACK.

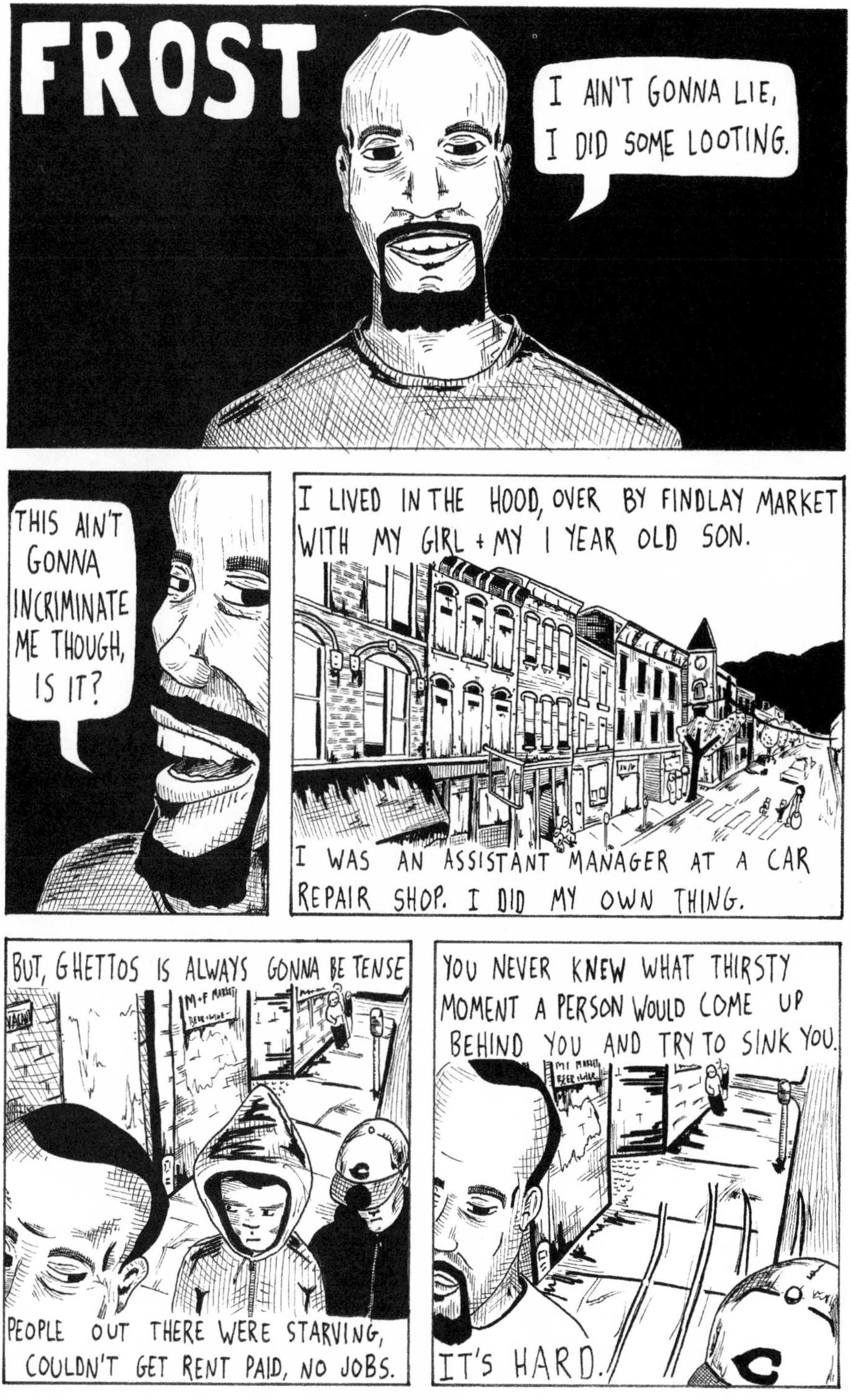
FROST
I AIN'T GONNA LIE, I DID SOME LOOTING.
THIS AIN'T GONNA INCRIMINATE ME THOUGH, IS IT?
I LIVED IN THE HOOD, OVER BY FINDLAY MARKET WITH MY GIRL + MY 1 YEAR OLD SON.
I WAS AN ASSISTANT MANAGER AT A CAR REPAIR SHOP. I DID MY OWN THING.
BUT, GHETTOS IS ALWAYS GONNA BE TENSE
PEOPLE OUT THERE WERE STARVING, COULDN'T GET RENT PAID, NO JOBS.
YOU NEVER KNEW WHAT THIRSTY MOMENT A PERSON WOULD COME UP BEHIND YOU AND TRY TO SINK YOU.
IT'S HARD.

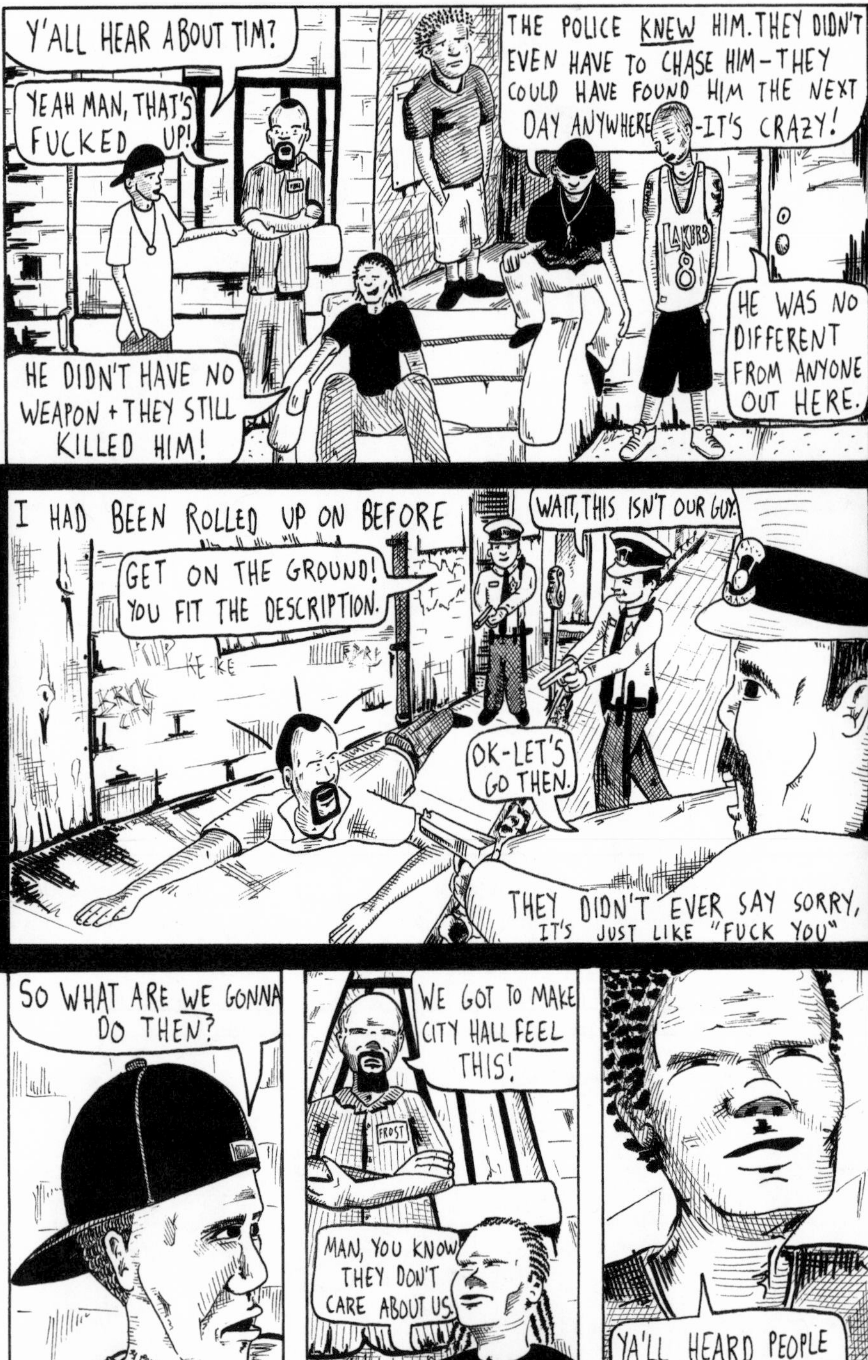
Y'ALL HEAR ABOUT TIM?
YEAH MAN, THAT'S FUCKED UP!
THE POLICE KNEW HIM. THEY DIDN'T EVEN HAVE TO CHASE HIM – THEY COULD HAVE FOUND HIM THE NEXT DAY ANYWHERE – IT'S CRAZY!
HE DIDN'T HAVE NO WEAPON + THEY STILL KILLED HIM!
HE WAS NO DIFFERENT FROM ANYONE OUT HERE.
I HAD BEEN ROLLED UP ON BEFORE
GET ON THE GROUND! YOU FIT THE DESCRIPTION.
WAIT, THIS ISN'T OUR GUY.
OK-LET'S GO THEN.
THEY DIDN'T EVER SAY SORRY, IT'S JUST LIKE "FUCK YOU"
SO WHAT ARE WE GONNA DO THEN?
WE GOT TO MAKE CITY HALL FEEL THIS!
FROST
MAN, YOU KNOW THEY DON'T CARE ABOUT US.
YA'LL HEARD PEOPLE IS LOOTING, RIGHT?

YEAH, BUT THESE STORES AIN'T GOT NOTHING TO DO WITH THIS.

NO, BUT THAT MIGHT WORK. WE COULD MAKE A STATEMENT. THEY'D HEAR US THEN. AND BESIDES, THESE STORES GOT INSURANCE.

WHO'S IN FOR TOMORROW?

HA HA

F'REAL THOUGH, I COULD USE A NEW SHIRT.

WE MET UP THE NEXT NIGHT IN MADISONVILLE

WE ALL WORE BLACK

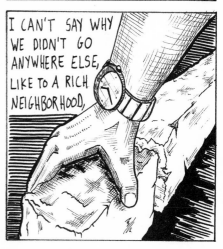

I CAN'T SAY WHY WE DIDN'T GO ANYWHERE ELSE, LIKE TO A RICH NEIGHBORHOOD,

WE JUST DIDN'T THINK ABOUT IT

DEVEROES

$2.99

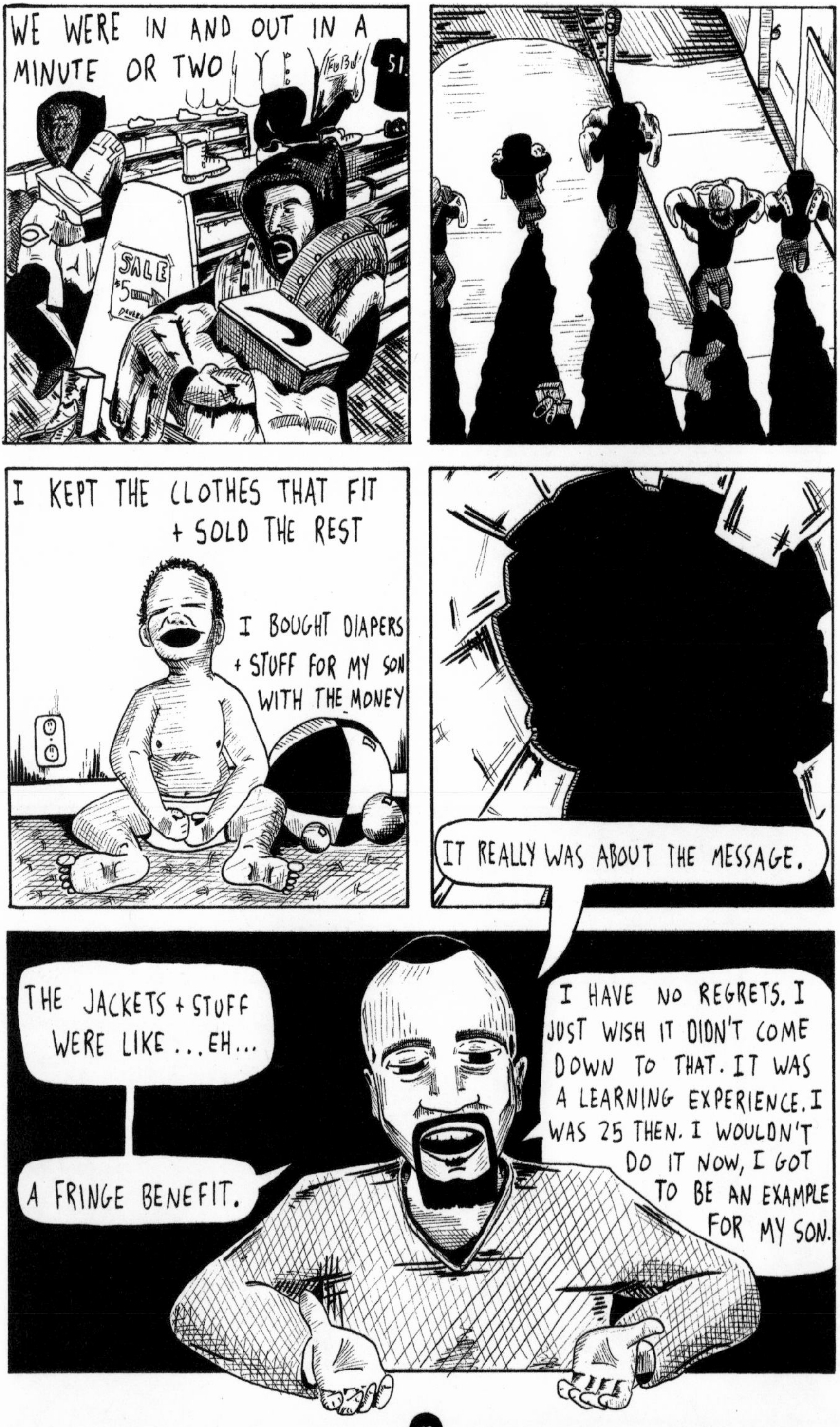
WE WERE IN AND OUT IN A MINUTE OR TWO
SALE $5
I KEPT THE CLOTHES THAT FIT + SOLD THE REST
I BOUGHT DIAPERS + STUFF FOR MY SON WITH THE MONEY
IT REALLY WAS ABOUT THE MESSAGE.
THE JACKETS + STUFF WERE LIKE... EH...
A FRINGE BENEFIT.
I HAVE NO REGRETS. I JUST WISH IT DIDN'T COME DOWN TO THAT. IT WAS A LEARNING EXPERIENCE. I WAS 25 THEN. I WOULDN'T DO IT NOW, I GOT TO BE AN EXAMPLE FOR MY SON.

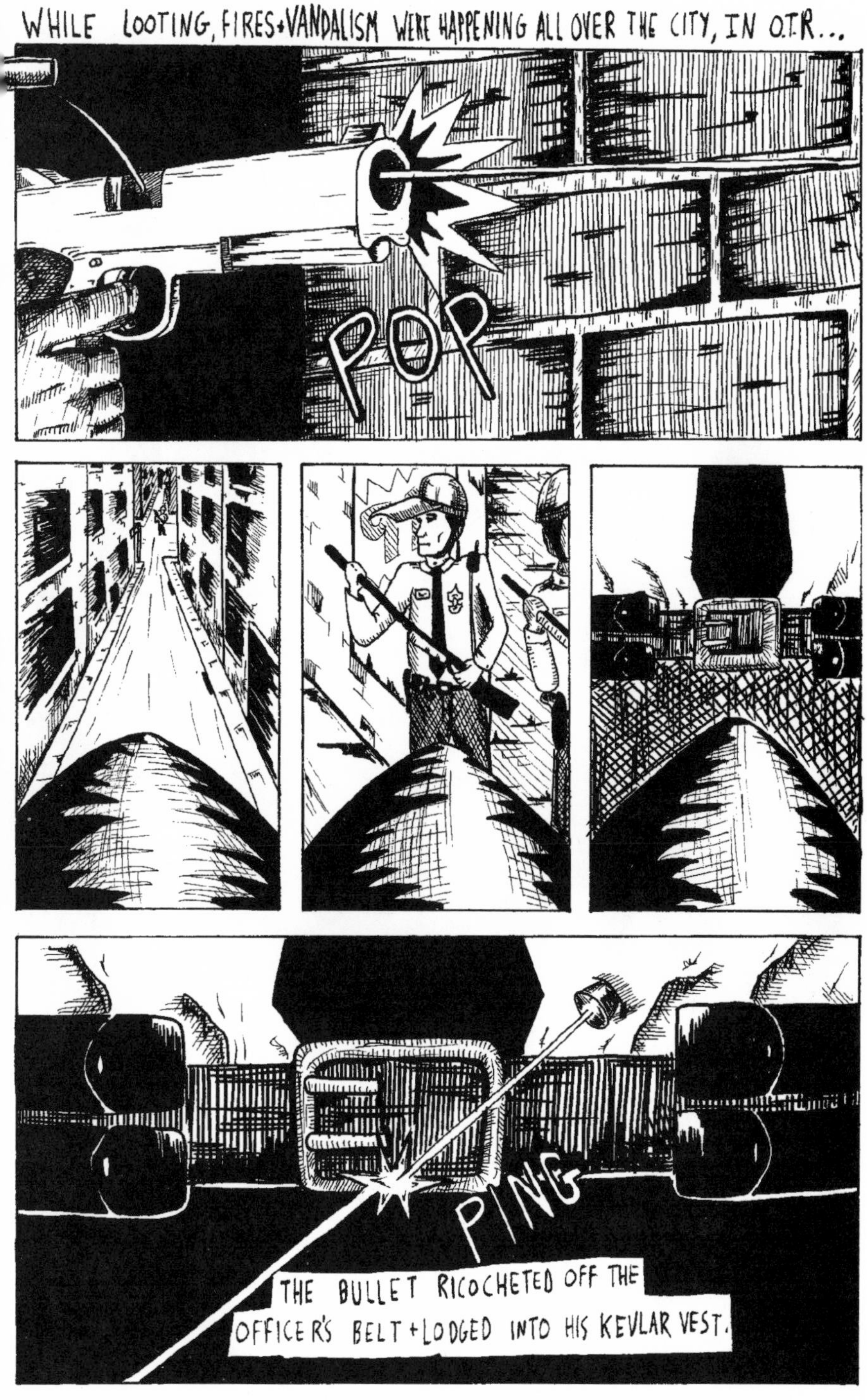
WHILE LOOTING, FIRES + VANDALISM WERE HAPPENING ALL OVER THE CITY, IN O.T.R...
POP
PING
THE BULLET RICOCHETED OFF THE OFFICER'S BELT + LODGED INTO HIS KEVLAR VEST.

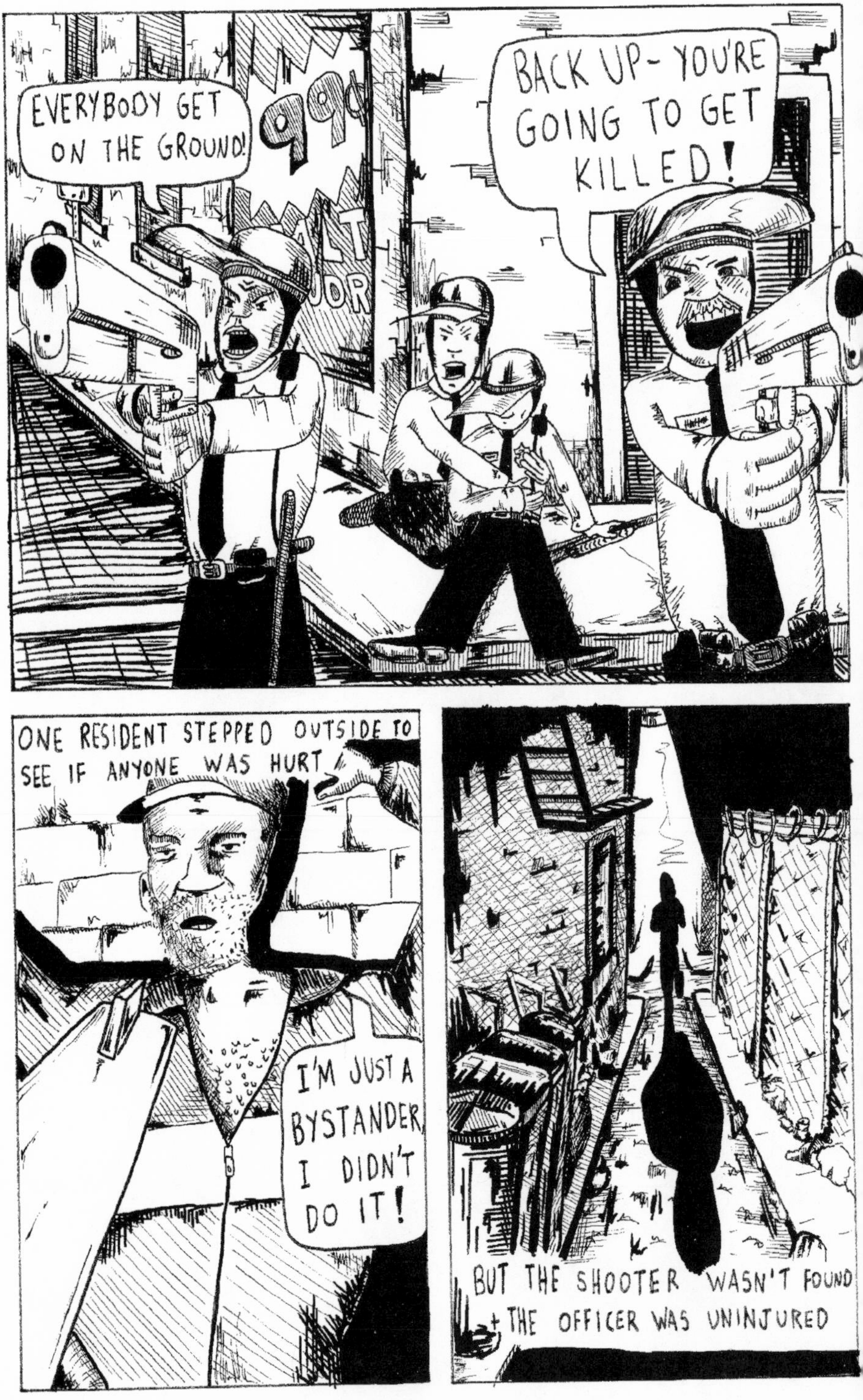
EVERYBODY GET ON THE GROUND!
99¢
BACK UP- YOU'RE GOING TO GET KILLED!
ONE RESIDENT STEPPED OUTSIDE TO SEE IF ANYONE WAS HURT
I'M JUST A BYSTANDER, I DIDN'T DO IT!
BUT THE SHOOTER WASN'T FOUND + THE OFFICER WAS UNINJURED

THURSDAY

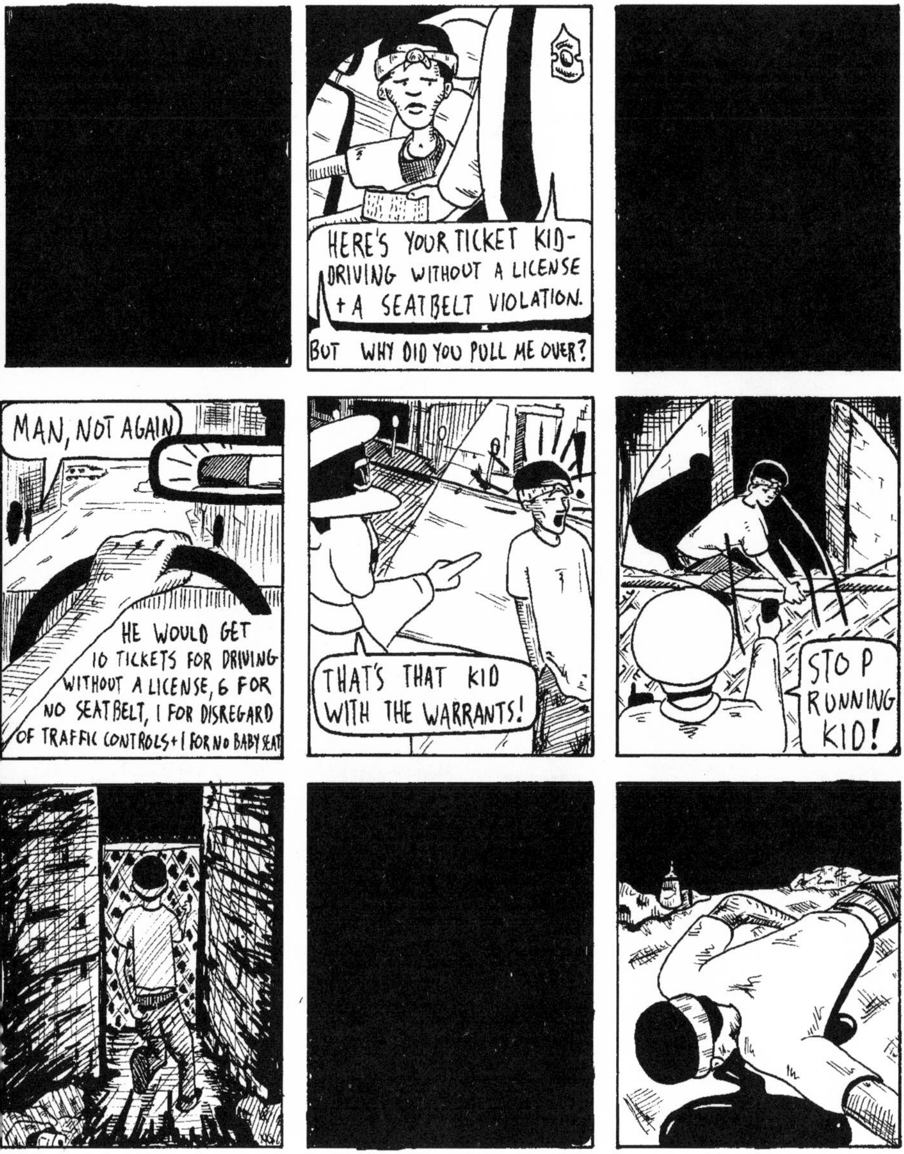
HERE'S YOUR TICKET KID-DRIVING WITHOUT A LICENSE + A SEATBELT VIOLATION.
BUT WHY DID YOU PULL ME OVER?
MAN, NOT AGAIN
HE WOULD GET 10 TICKETS FOR DRIVING WITHOUT A LICENSE, 6 FOR NO SEATBELT, 1 FOR DISREGARD OF TRAFFIC CONTROLS + 1 FOR NO BABY SEAT
THAT'S THAT KID WITH THE WARRANTS!
STOP RUNNING KID!

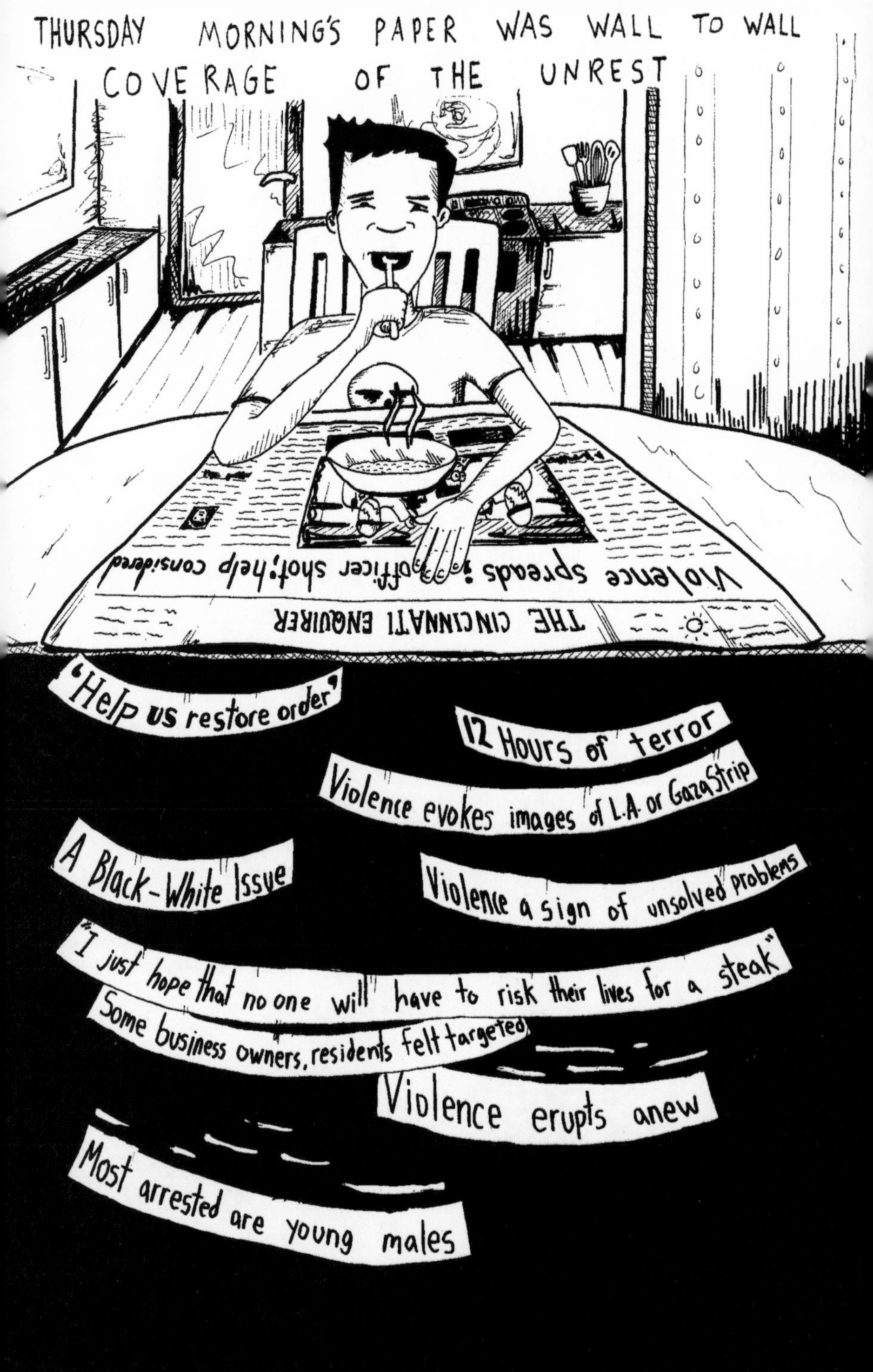
THURSDAY MORNING'S PAPER WAS WALL TO WALL COVERAGE OF THE UNREST
Violence spreads: officer shot; help considered
THE CINCINNATI ENQUIRER
'Help us restore order'
12 Hours of terror
Violence evokes images of L.A. or Gaza Strip
A Black-White Issue
Violence a sign of unsolved problems
"I just hope that no one will have to risk their lives for a steak"
Some business owners, residents felt targeted
Violence erupts anew
Most arrested are young males

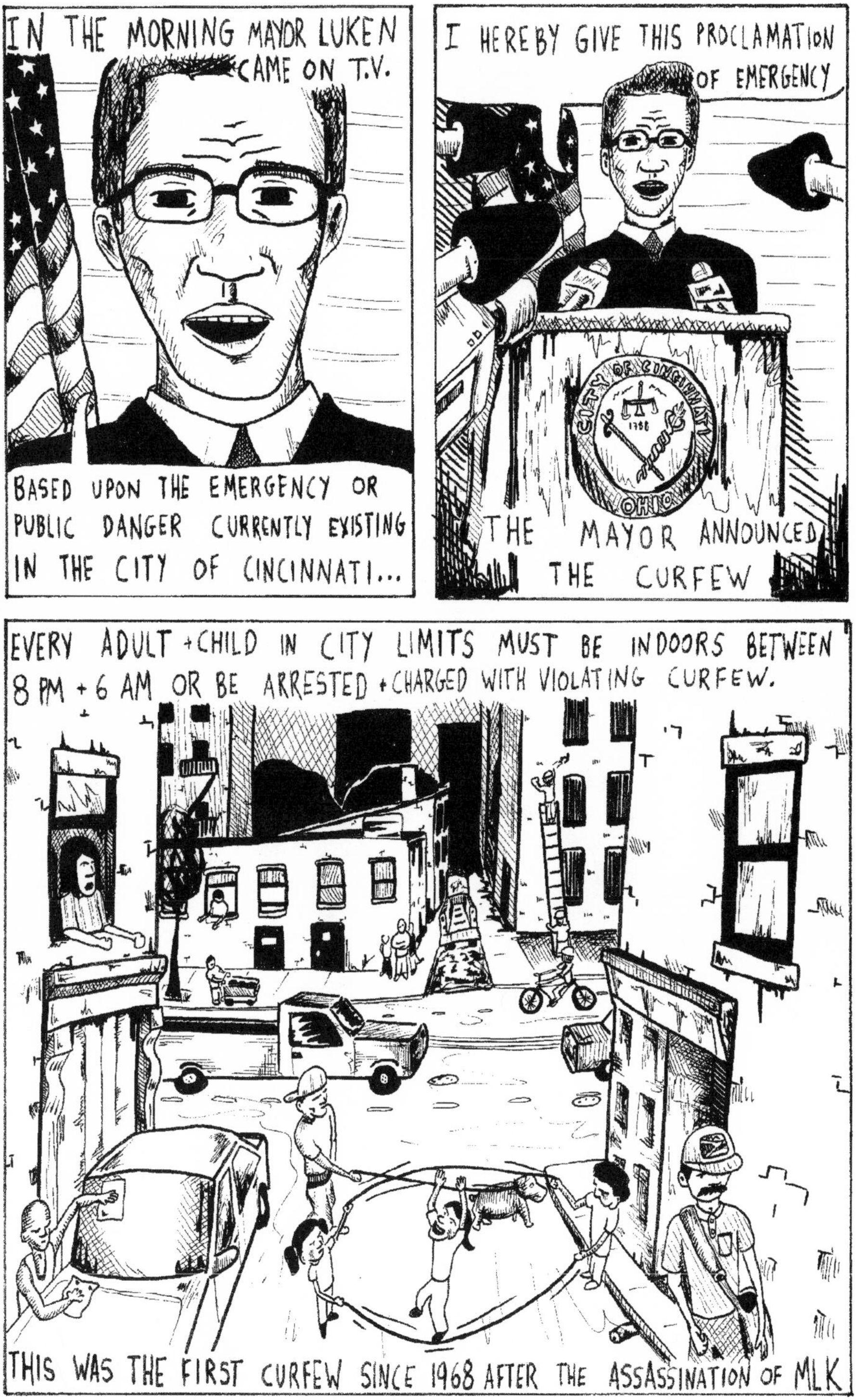
IN THE MORNING MAYOR LUKEN CAME ON T.V.
BASED UPON THE EMERGENCY OR PUBLIC DANGER CURRENTLY EXISTING IN THE CITY OF CINCINNATI...
I HEREBY GIVE THIS PROCLAMATION OF EMERGENCY
CITY OF CINCINNATI
1788
OHIO
THE MAYOR ANNOUNCED THE CURFEW
EVERY ADULT + CHILD IN CITY LIMITS MUST BE INDOORS BETWEEN 8 PM + 6 AM OR BE ARRESTED + CHARGED WITH VIOLATING CURFEW.
THIS WAS THE FIRST CURFEW SINCE 1968 AFTER THE ASSASSINATION OF MLK

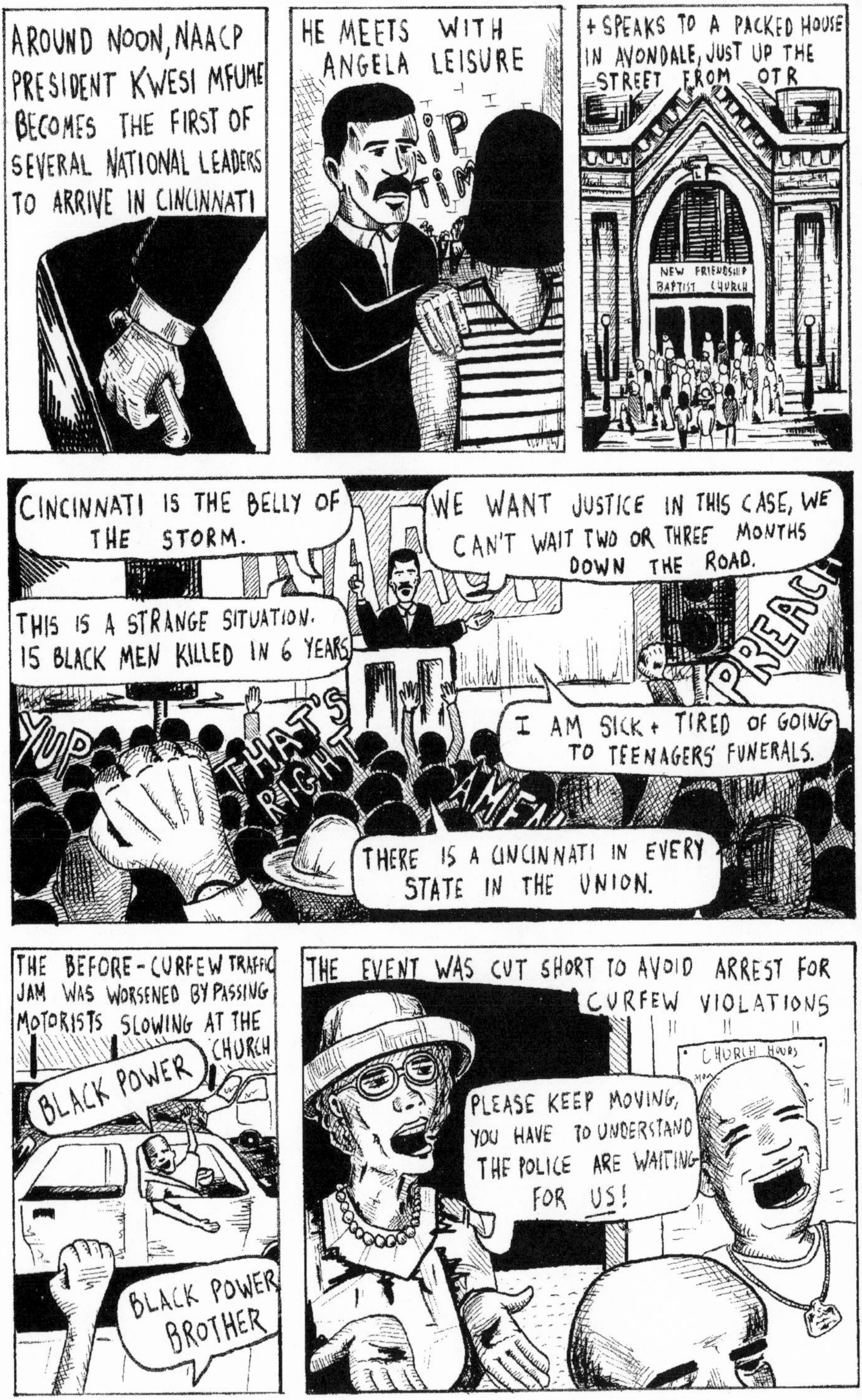
AROUND NOON, NAACP PRESIDENT KWESI MFUME BECOMES THE FIRST OF SEVERAL NATIONAL LEADERS TO ARRIVE IN CINCINNATI
HE MEETS WITH ANGELA LEISURE
+ SPEAKS TO A PACKED HOUSE IN AVONDALE, JUST UP THE STREET FROM OTR
NEW FRIENDSHIP BAPTIST CHURCH
CINCINNATI IS THE BELLY OF THE STORM.
WE WANT JUSTICE IN THIS CASE, WE CAN'T WAIT TWO OR THREE MONTHS DOWN THE ROAD.
PREACH
THIS IS A STRANGE SITUATION. 15 BLACK MEN KILLED IN 6 YEARS
YUP
THAT'S RIGHT
I AM SICK + TIRED OF GOING TO TEENAGERS' FUNERALS.
AMEN
THERE IS A CINCINNATI IN EVERY STATE IN THE UNION.
THE BEFORE-CURFEW TRAFFIC JAM WAS WORSENED BY PASSING MOTORISTS SLOWING AT THE CHURCH
BLACK POWER
BLACK POWER BROTHER
THE EVENT WAS CUT SHORT TO AVOID ARREST FOR CURFEW VIOLATIONS
CHURCH HOURS
PLEASE KEEP MOVING, YOU HAVE TO UNDERSTAND THE POLICE ARE WAITING FOR US!

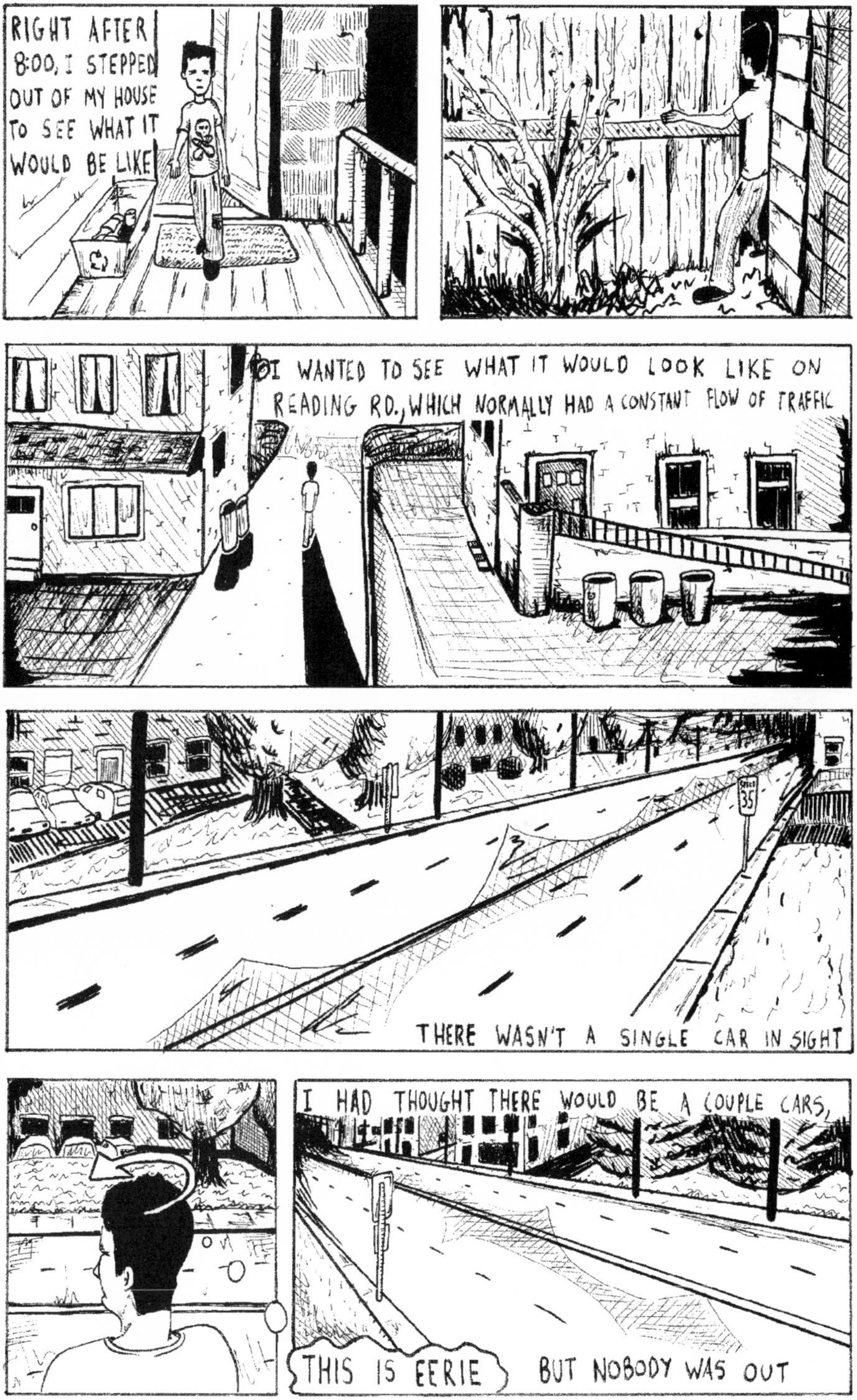
RIGHT AFTER 8:00, I STEPPED OUT OF MY HOUSE TO SEE WHAT IT WOULD BE LIKE
I WANTED TO SEE WHAT IT WOULD LOOK LIKE ON READING RD., WHICH NORMALLY HAD A CONSTANT FLOW OF TRAFFIC
35
THERE WASN'T A SINGLE CAR IN SIGHT
I HAD THOUGHT THERE WOULD BE A COUPLE CARS,
THIS IS EERIE
BUT NOBODY WAS OUT

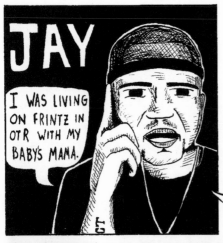

JAY

I WAS LIVING ON FRINTZ IN OTR WITH MY BABY'S MAMA.

EMPLOYEE

CLUNK

I WAS WORKING AS A COOK AT THE BENGALS' STADIUM + GOT OFF A LONG SHIFT.

WHERE'S EVERYBODY AT?

FREEZE, DON'T MOVE.

OLICE

SCREECH

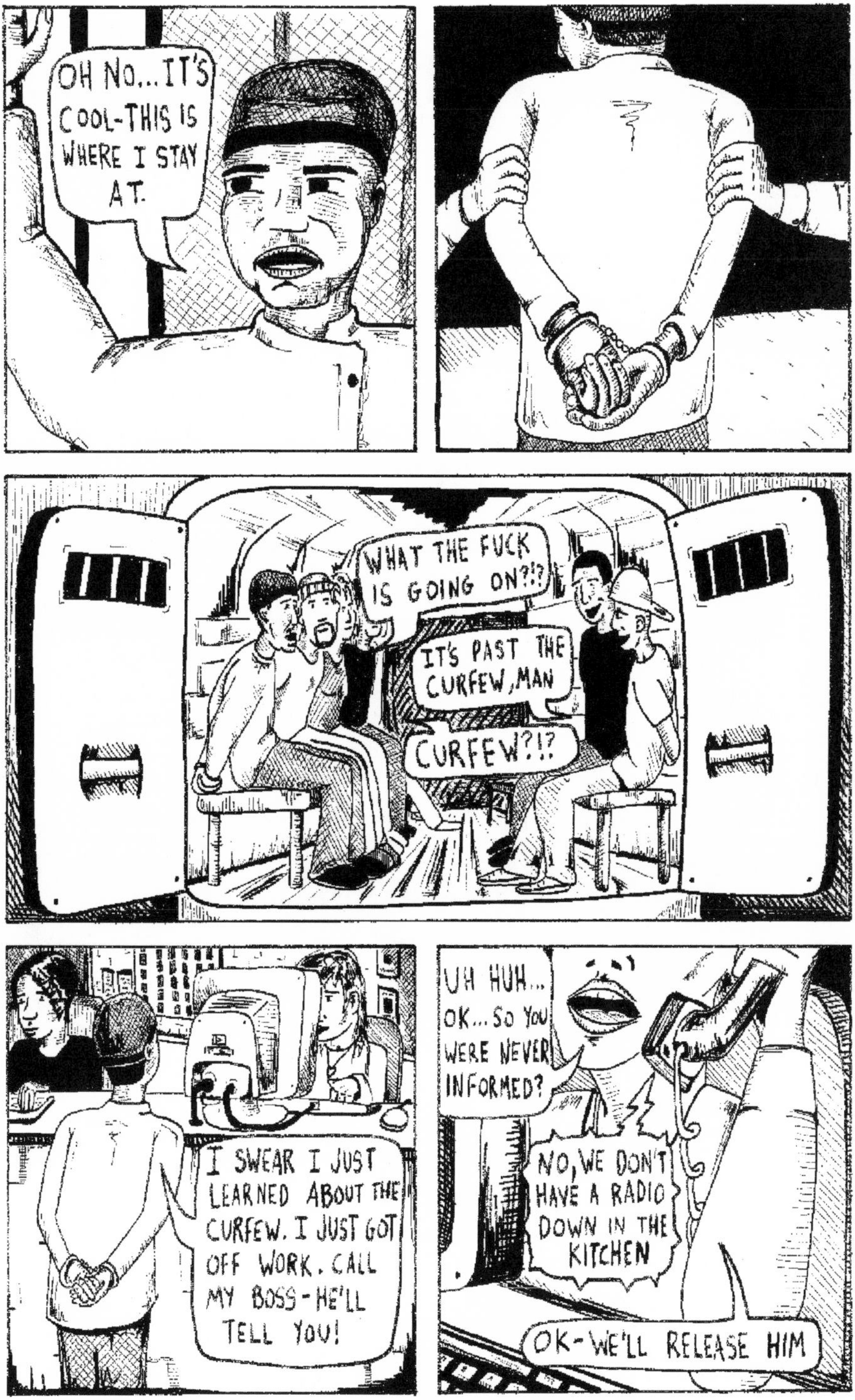
OH NO... IT'S COOL-THIS IS WHERE I STAY AT.
WHAT THE FUCK IS GOING ON?!?
IT'S PAST THE CURFEW, MAN
CURFEW?!?
I SWEAR I JUST LEARNED ABOUT THE CURFEW. I JUST GOT OFF WORK. CALL MY BOSS-HE'LL TELL YOU!
UH HUH... OK... SO YOU WERE NEVER INFORMED?
NO, WE DON'T HAVE A RADIO DOWN IN THE KITCHEN
OK-WE'LL RELEASE HIM

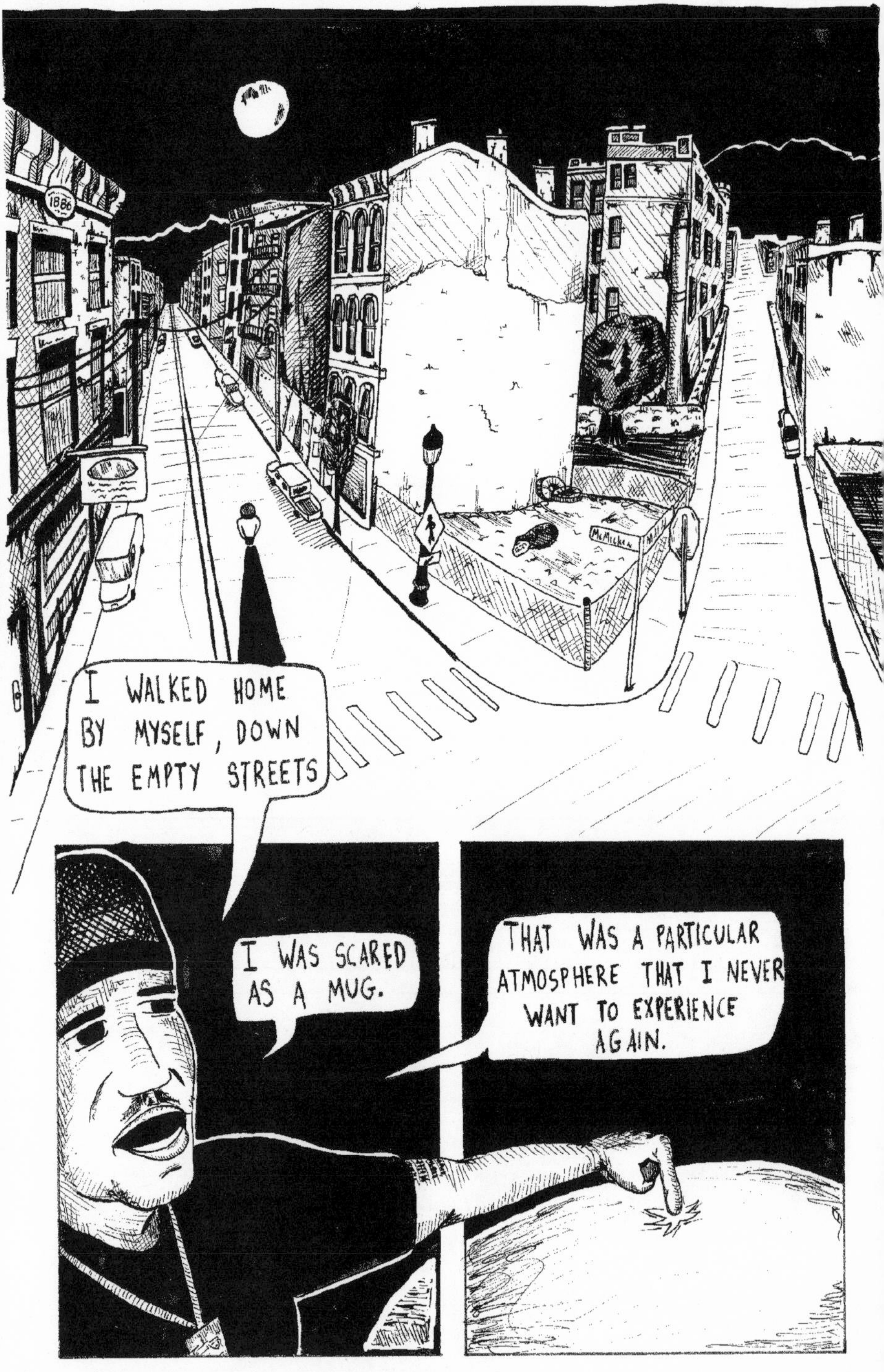
1886
McMicken
I WALKED HOME BY MYSELF, DOWN THE EMPTY STREETS
I WAS SCARED AS A MUG.
THAT WAS A PARTICULAR ATMOSPHERE THAT I NEVER WANT TO EXPERIENCE AGAIN.

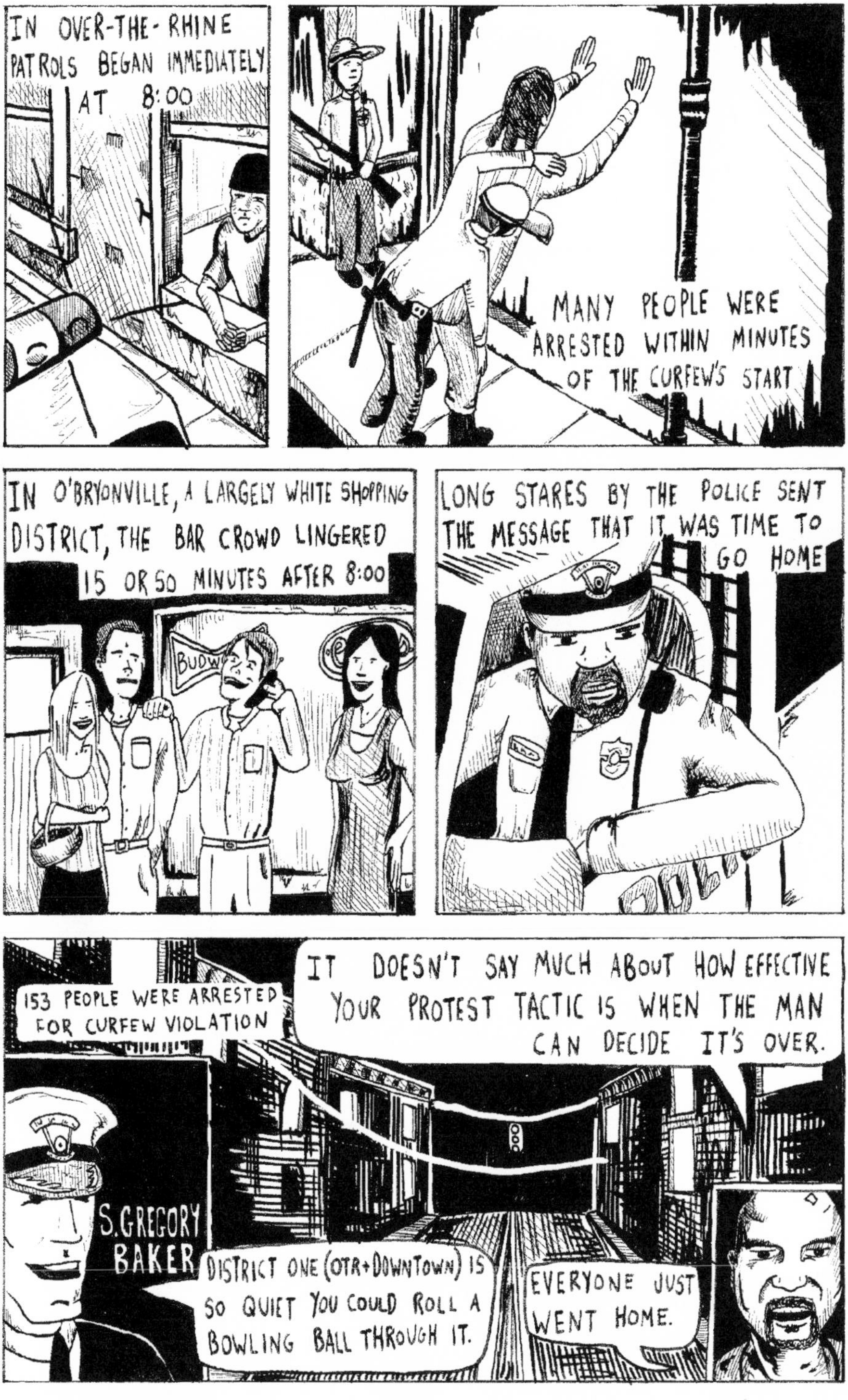
IN OVER-THE-RHINE PATROLS BEGAN IMMEDIATELY AT 8:00
MANY PEOPLE WERE ARRESTED WITHIN MINUTES OF THE CURFEW'S START
IN O'BRYONVILLE, A LARGELY WHITE SHOPPING DISTRICT, THE BAR CROWD LINGERED 15 OR SO MINUTES AFTER 8:00
LONG STARES BY THE POLICE SENT THE MESSAGE THAT IT WAS TIME TO GO HOME
153 PEOPLE WERE ARRESTED FOR CURFEW VIOLATION
IT DOESN'T SAY MUCH ABOUT HOW EFFECTIVE YOUR PROTEST TACTIC IS WHEN THE MAN CAN DECIDE IT'S OVER.
S.GREGORY BAKER
DISTRICT ONE (OTR+DOWNTOWN) IS SO QUIET YOU COULD ROLL A BOWLING BALL THROUGH IT.
EVERYONE JUST WENT HOME.

FRIDAY

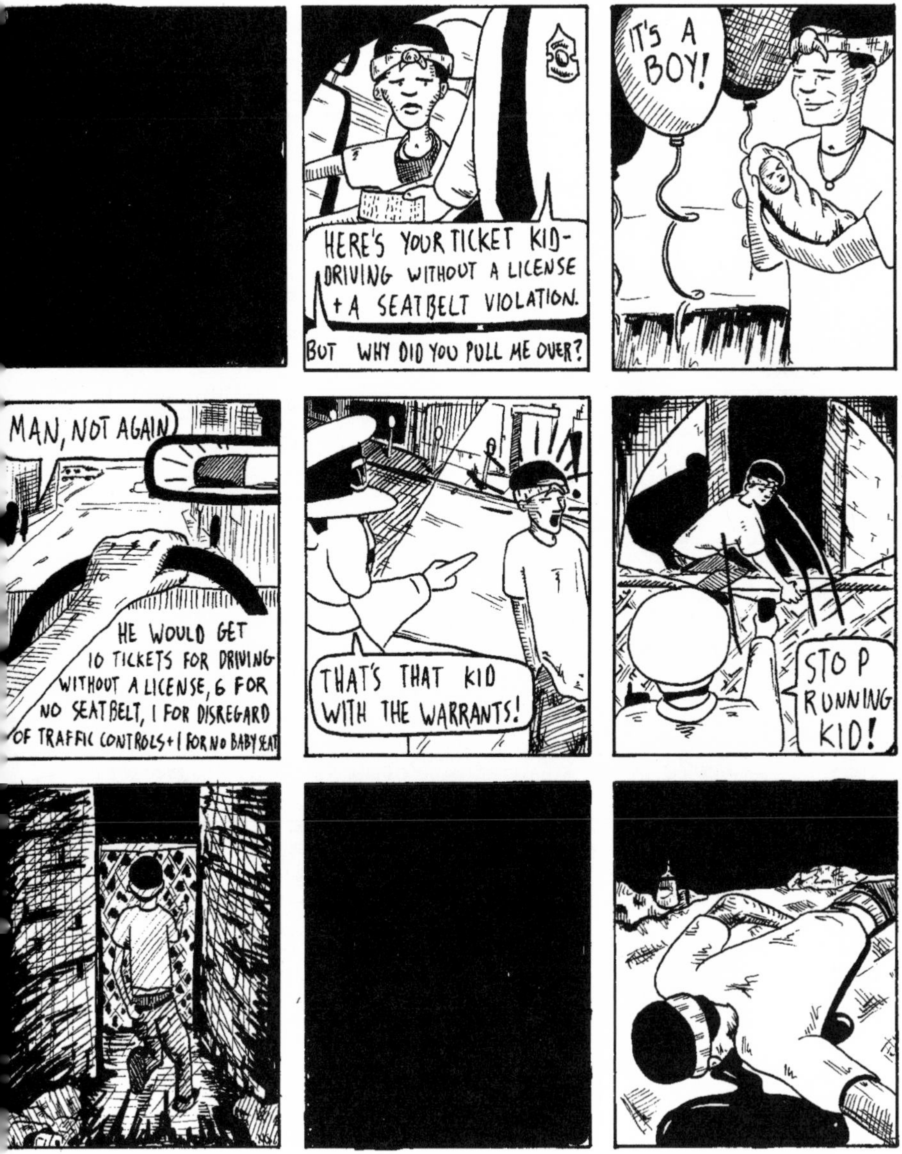
HERE'S YOUR TICKET KID-DRIVING WITHOUT A LICENSE + A SEATBELT VIOLATION.
BUT WHY DID YOU PULL ME OVER?
IT'S A BOY!
MAN, NOT AGAIN
HE WOULD GET 10 TICKETS FOR DRIVING WITHOUT A LICENSE, 6 FOR NO SEATBELT, 1 FOR DISREGARD OF TRAFFIC CONTROLS + 1 FOR NO BABY SEAT
THAT'S THAT KID WITH THE WARRANTS!
STOP RUNNING KID!

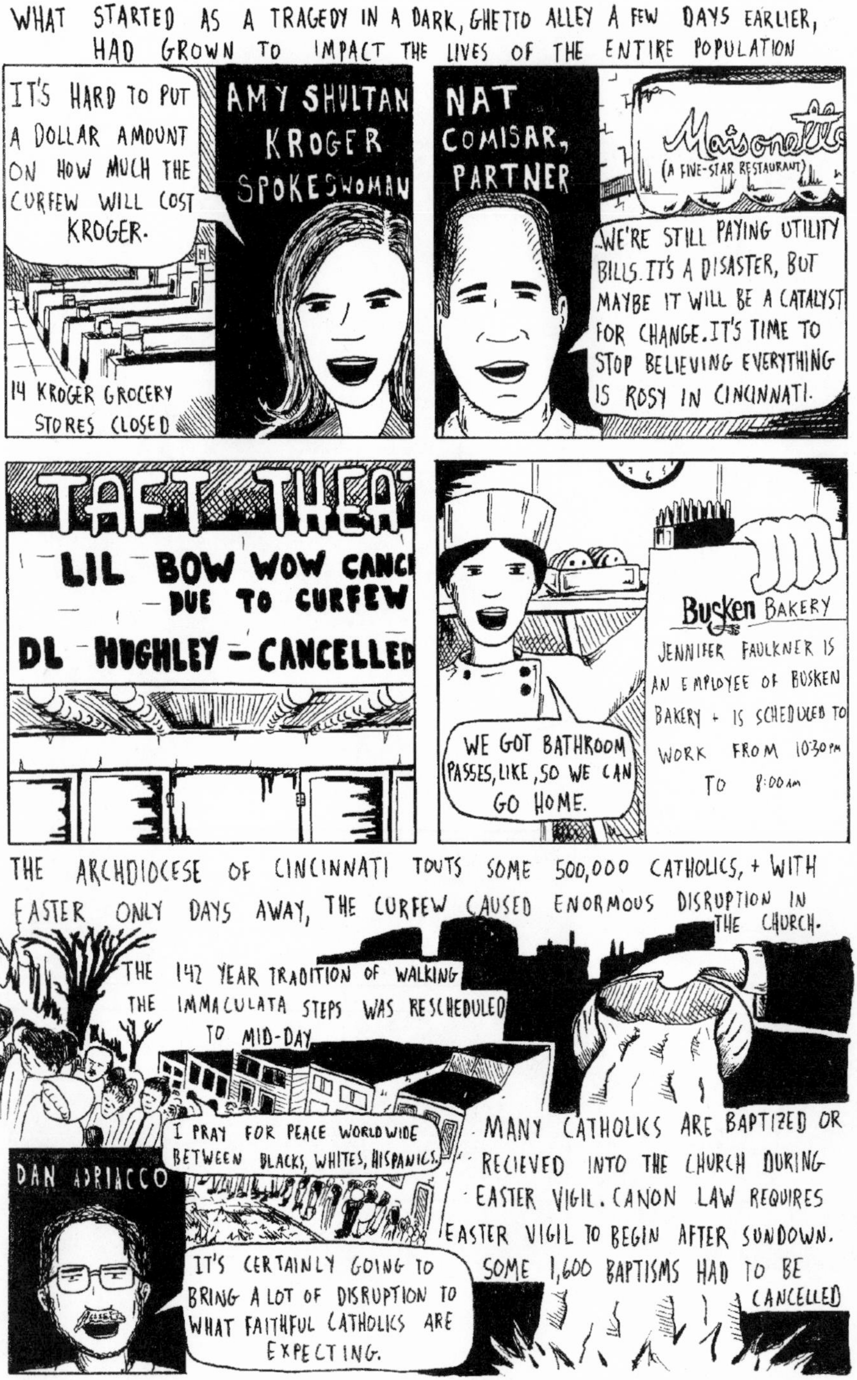
WHAT STARTED AS A TRAGEDY IN A DARK, GHETTO ALLEY A FEW DAYS EARLIER, HAD GROWN TO IMPACT THE LIVES OF THE ENTIRE POPULATION
IT'S HARD TO PUT A DOLLAR AMOUNT ON HOW MUCH THE CURFEW WILL COST KROGER.
AMY SHULTAN KROGER SPOKESWOMAN
14 KROGER GROCERY STORES CLOSED
14
NAT COMISAR, PARTNER
Maisonette
(A FIVE-STAR RESTAURANT)
WE'RE STILL PAYING UTILITY BILLS. IT'S A DISASTER, BUT MAYBE IT WILL BE A CATALYST FOR CHANGE. IT'S TIME TO STOP BELIEVING EVERYTHING IS ROSY IN CINCINNATI.
TAFT THEAT
LIL BOW WOW CANC
DUE TO CURFEW
DL HUGHLEY - CANCELLED
Busken BAKERY
JENNIFER FAULKNER IS AN EMPLOYEE OF BUSKEN BAKERY + IS SCHEDULED TO WORK FROM 10:30PM TO 8:00AM
WE GOT BATHROOM PASSES, LIKE, SO WE CAN GO HOME.
THE ARCHDIOCESE OF CINCINNATI TOUTS SOME 500,000 CATHOLICS, + WITH EASTER ONLY DAYS AWAY, THE CURFEW CAUSED ENORMOUS DISRUPTION IN THE CHURCH.
THE 142 YEAR TRADITION OF WALKING THE IMMACULATA STEPS WAS RESCHEDULED TO MID-DAY
I PRAY FOR PEACE WORLDWIDE BETWEEN BLACKS, WHITES, HISPANICS.
DAN ADRIACCO
IT'S CERTAINLY GOING TO BRING A LOT OF DISRUPTION TO WHAT FAITHFUL CATHOLICS ARE EXPECTING.
MANY CATHOLICS ARE BAPTIZED OR RECIEVED INTO THE CHURCH DURING EASTER VIGIL. CANON LAW REQUIRES EASTER VIGIL TO BEGIN AFTER SUNDOWN. SOME 1,600 BAPTISMS HAD TO BE CANCELLED

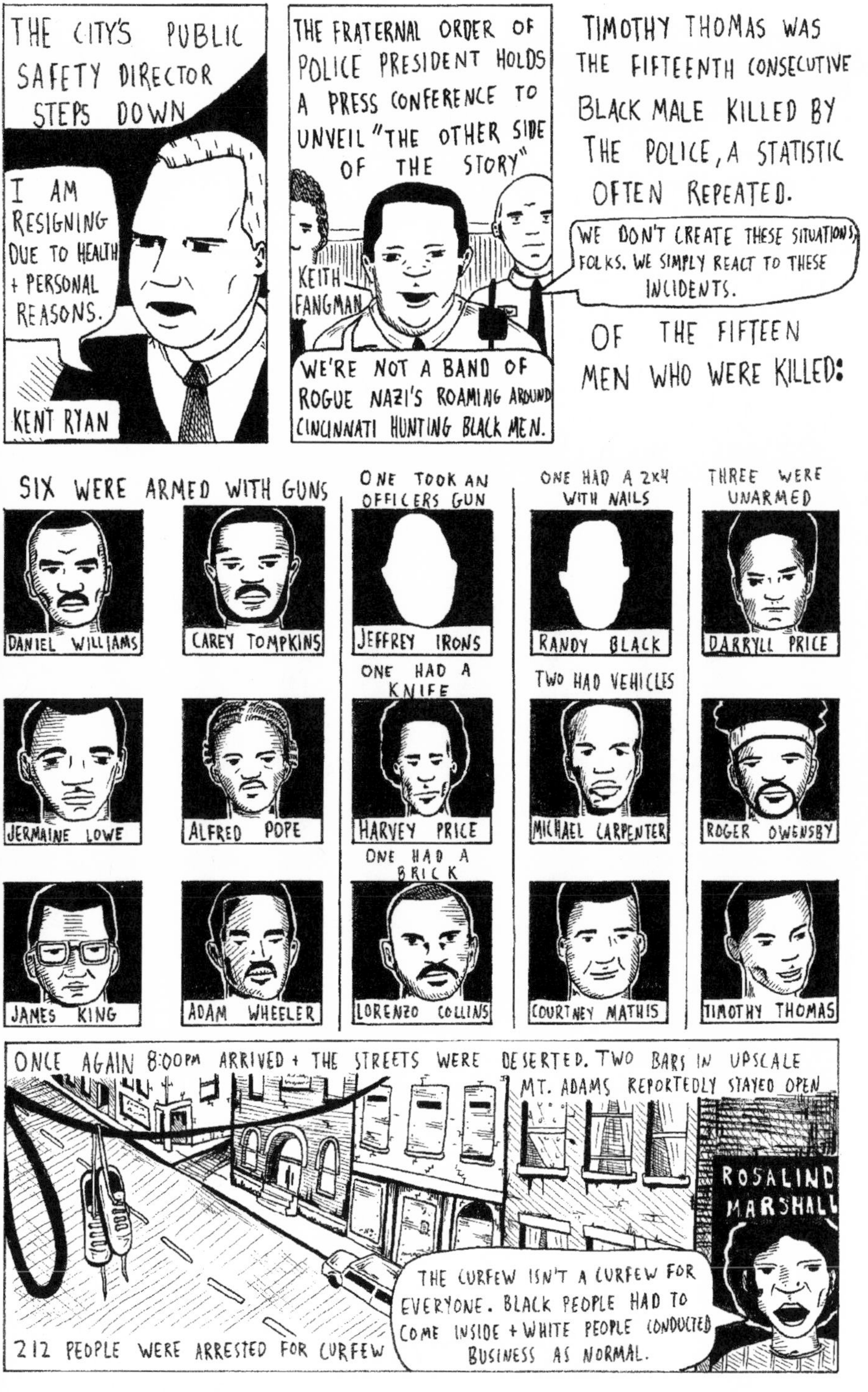
THE CITY'S PUBLIC SAFETY DIRECTOR STEPS DOWN
I AM RESIGNING DUE TO HEALTH + PERSONAL REASONS.
KENT RYAN
THE FRATERNAL ORDER OF POLICE PRESIDENT HOLDS A PRESS CONFERENCE TO UNVEIL "THE OTHER SIDE OF THE STORY"
KEITH FANGMAN
WE'RE NOT A BAND OF ROGUE NAZI'S ROAMING AROUND CINCINNATI HUNTING BLACK MEN.
WE DON'T CREATE THESE SITUATIONS, FOLKS. WE SIMPLY REACT TO THESE INCIDENTS.
TIMOTHY THOMAS WAS THE FIFTEENTH CONSECUTIVE BLACK MALE KILLED BY THE POLICE, A STATISTIC OFTEN REPEATED.
OF THE FIFTEEN MEN WHO WERE KILLED:
SIX WERE ARMED WITH GUNS
DANIEL WILLIAMS
CAREY TOMPKINS
JERMAINE LOWE
ALFRED POPE
JAMES KING
ADAM WHEELER
ONE TOOK AN OFFICERS GUN
JEFFREY IRONS
ONE HAD A KNIFE
HARVEY PRICE
ONE HAD A BRICK
LORENZO COLLINS
ONE HAD A 2x4 WITH NAILS
RANDY BLACK
TWO HAD VEHICLES
MICHAEL CARPENTER
COURTNEY MATHIS
THREE WERE UNARMED
DARRYLL PRICE
ROGER OWENSBY
TIMOTHY THOMAS
ONCE AGAIN 8:00PM ARRIVED + THE STREETS WERE DESERTED. TWO BARS IN UPSCALE MT. ADAMS REPORTEDLY STAYED OPEN
ROSALIND MARSHALL
THE CURFEW ISN'T A CURFEW FOR EVERYONE. BLACK PEOPLE HAD TO COME INSIDE + WHITE PEOPLE CONDUCTED BUSINESS AS NORMAL.
212 PEOPLE WERE ARRESTED FOR CURFEW

SATURDAY

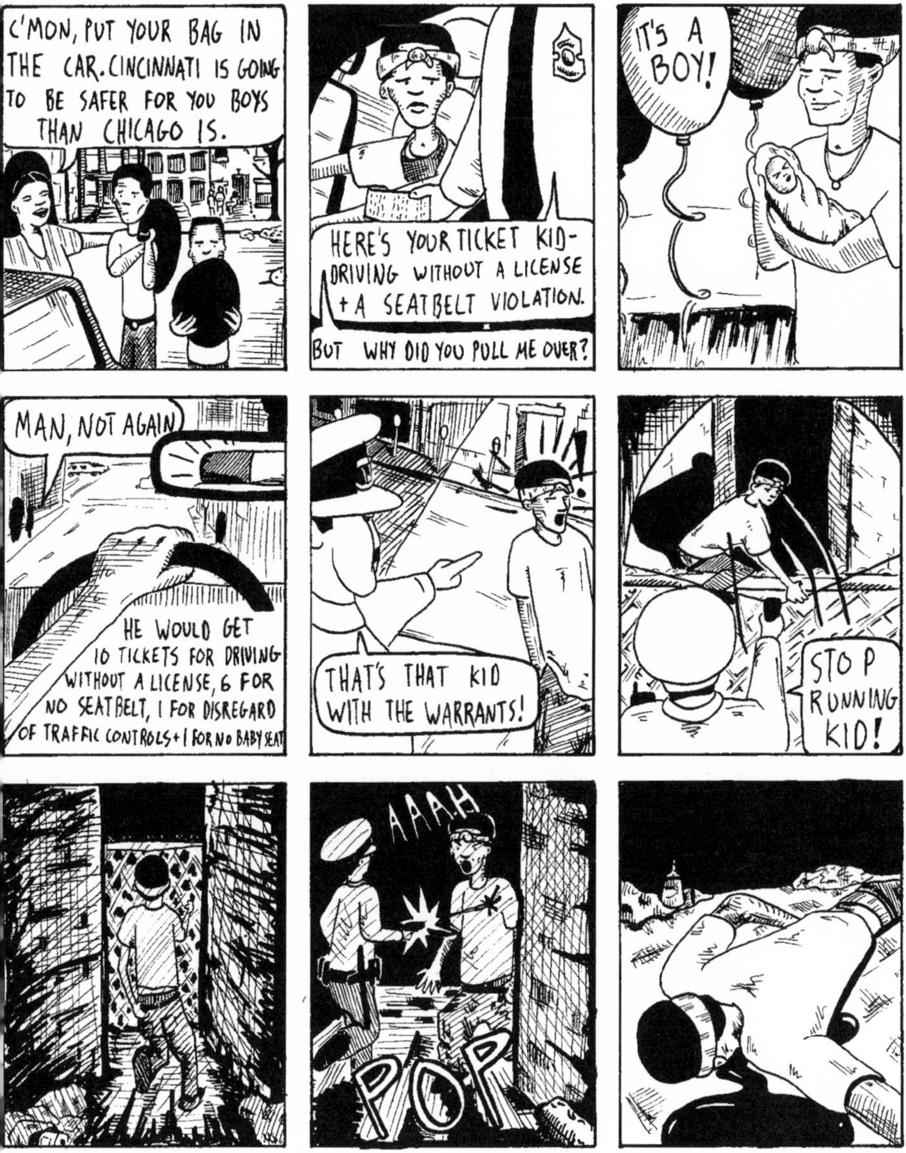
C'MON, PUT YOUR BAG IN THE CAR. CINCINNATI IS GOING TO BE SAFER FOR YOU BOYS THAN CHICAGO IS.
HERE'S YOUR TICKET KID- DRIVING WITHOUT A LICENSE + A SEATBELT VIOLATION.
BUT WHY DID YOU PULL ME OVER?
IT'S A BOY!
MAN, NOT AGAIN
HE WOULD GET 10 TICKETS FOR DRIVING WITHOUT A LICENSE, 6 FOR NO SEATBELT, 1 FOR DISREGARD OF TRAFFIC CONTROLS + 1 FOR NO BABY SEAT
THAT'S THAT KID WITH THE WARRANTS!
STOP RUNNING KID!
AAAH
POP

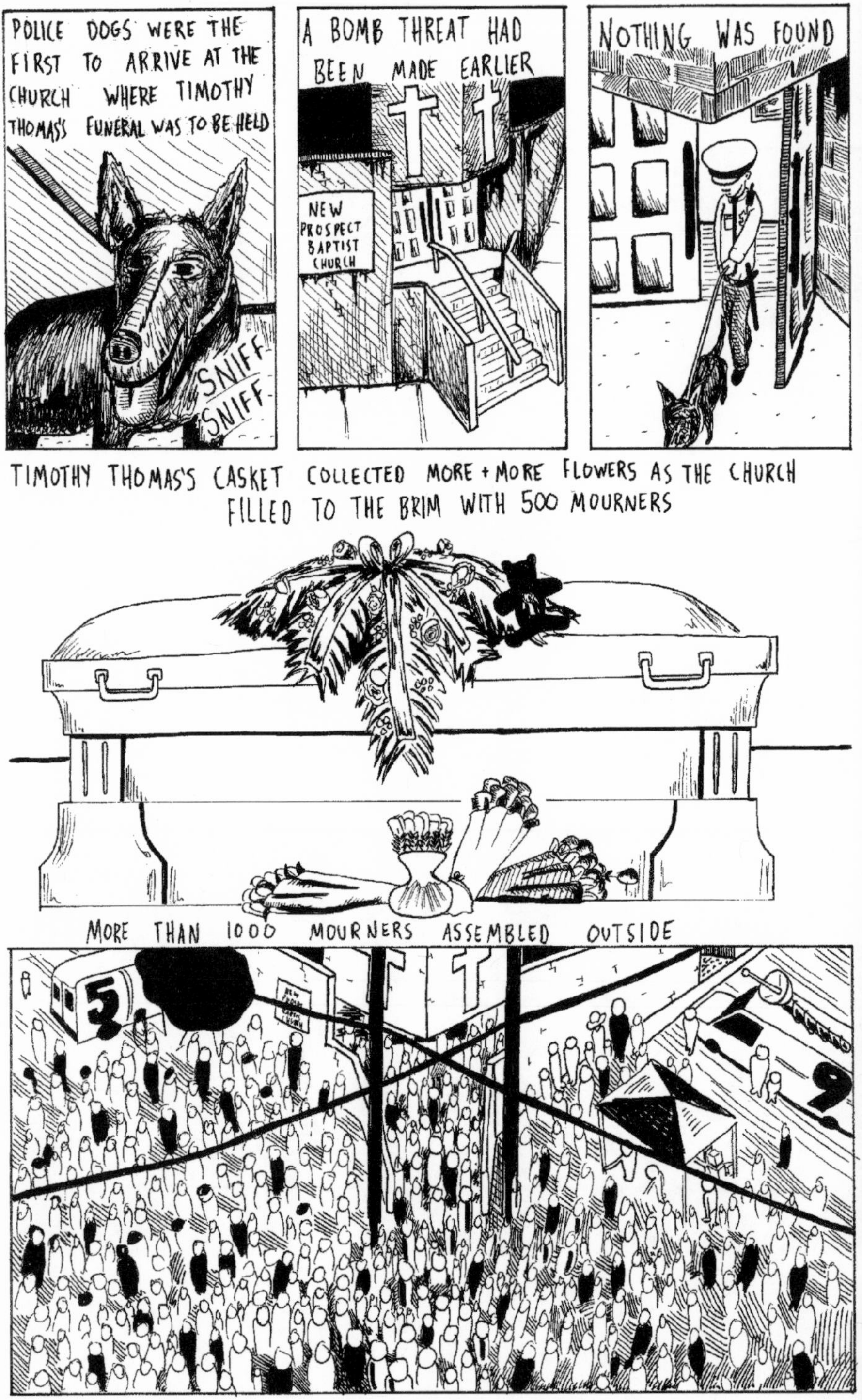
POLICE DOGS WERE THE FIRST TO ARRIVE AT THE CHURCH WHERE TIMOTHY THOMAS'S FUNERAL WAS TO BE HELD
SNIFF SNIFF
A BOMB THREAT HAD BEEN MADE EARLIER
NEW PROSPECT BAPTIST CHURCH
NOTHING WAS FOUND
TIMOTHY THOMAS'S CASKET COLLECTED MORE + MORE FLOWERS AS THE CHURCH FILLED TO THE BRIM WITH 500 MOURNERS
MORE THAN 1000 MOURNERS ASSEMBLED OUTSIDE

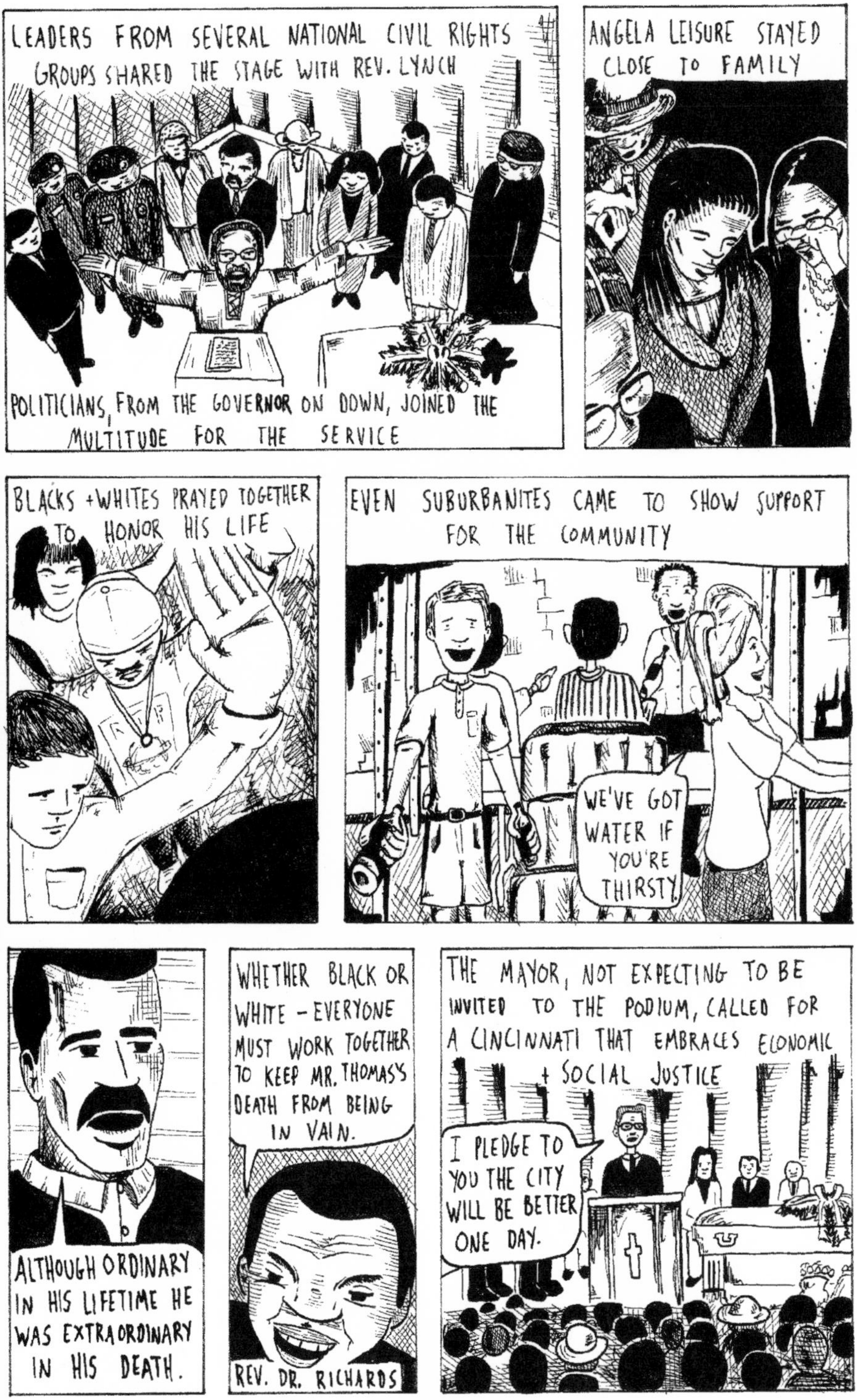
LEADERS FROM SEVERAL NATIONAL CIVIL RIGHTS GROUPS SHARED THE STAGE WITH REV. LYNCH
POLITICIANS, FROM THE GOVERNOR ON DOWN, JOINED THE MULTITUDE FOR THE SERVICE
ANGELA LEISURE STAYED CLOSE TO FAMILY
BLACKS + WHITES PRAYED TOGETHER TO HONOR HIS LIFE
EVEN SUBURBANITES CAME TO SHOW SUPPORT FOR THE COMMUNITY
WE'VE GOT WATER IF YOU'RE THIRSTY
ALTHOUGH ORDINARY IN HIS LIFETIME HE WAS EXTRAORDINARY IN HIS DEATH.
WHETHER BLACK OR WHITE - EVERYONE MUST WORK TOGETHER TO KEEP MR. THOMAS'S DEATH FROM BEING IN VAIN.
REV. DR. RICHARDS
THE MAYOR, NOT EXPECTING TO BE INVITED TO THE PODIUM, CALLED FOR A CINCINNATI THAT EMBRACES ECONOMIC + SOCIAL JUSTICE
I PLEDGE TO YOU THE CITY WILL BE BETTER ONE DAY.

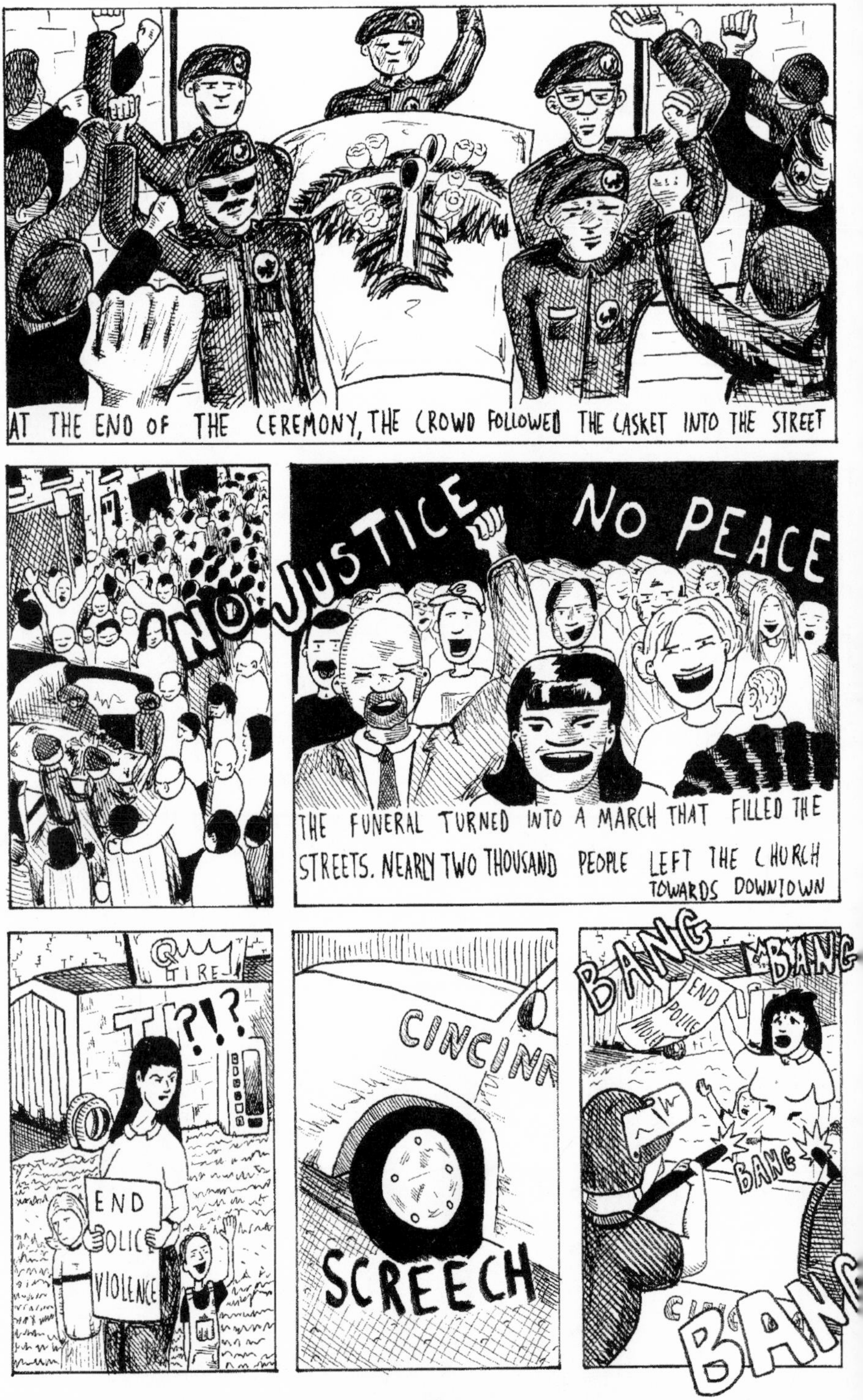
AT THE END OF THE CEREMONY, THE CROWD FOLLOWED THE CASKET INTO THE STREET
NO JUSTICE
NO PEACE
THE FUNERAL TURNED INTO A MARCH THAT FILLED THE STREETS. NEARLY TWO THOUSAND PEOPLE LEFT THE CHURCH TOWARDS DOWNTOWN
TIRE
END
OLIC
VIOLENCE
CINCINN
SCREECH
BANG
BANG
END
POLICE
BANG
BANG

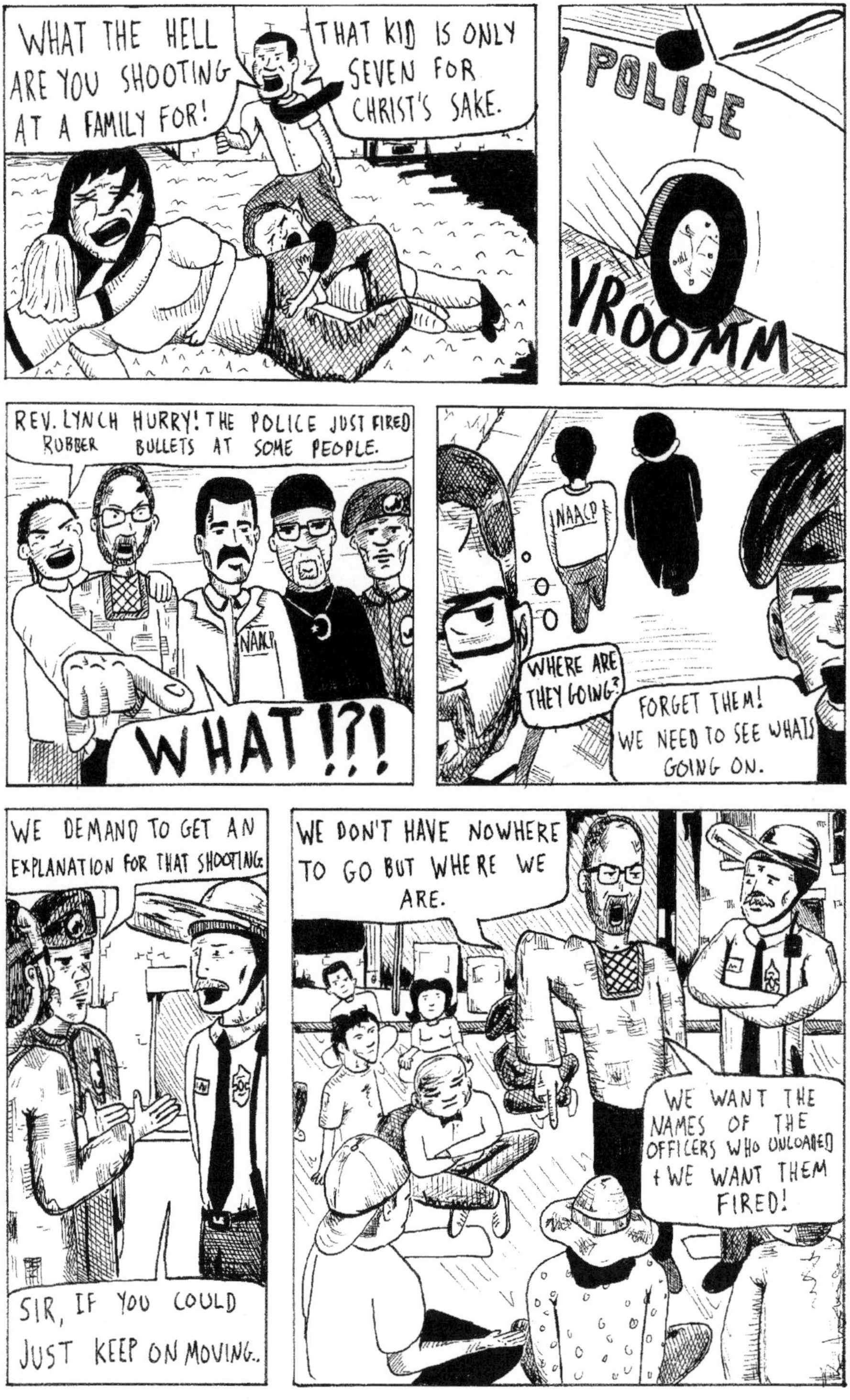
WHAT THE HELL ARE YOU SHOOTING AT A FAMILY FOR!
THAT KID IS ONLY SEVEN FOR CHRIST'S SAKE.
POLICE
VROOMM
REV. LYNCH HURRY! THE POLICE JUST FIRED RUBBER BULLETS AT SOME PEOPLE.
NAACP
WHAT!?!
NAACP
WHERE ARE THEY GOING?
FORGET THEM! WE NEED TO SEE WHATS GOING ON.
WE DEMAND TO GET AN EXPLANATION FOR THAT SHOOTING.
SIR, IF YOU COULD JUST KEEP ON MOVING..
WE DON'T HAVE NOWHERE TO GO BUT WHERE WE ARE.
NAACP
WE WANT THE NAMES OF THE OFFICERS WHO UNLOADED + WE WANT THEM FIRED!

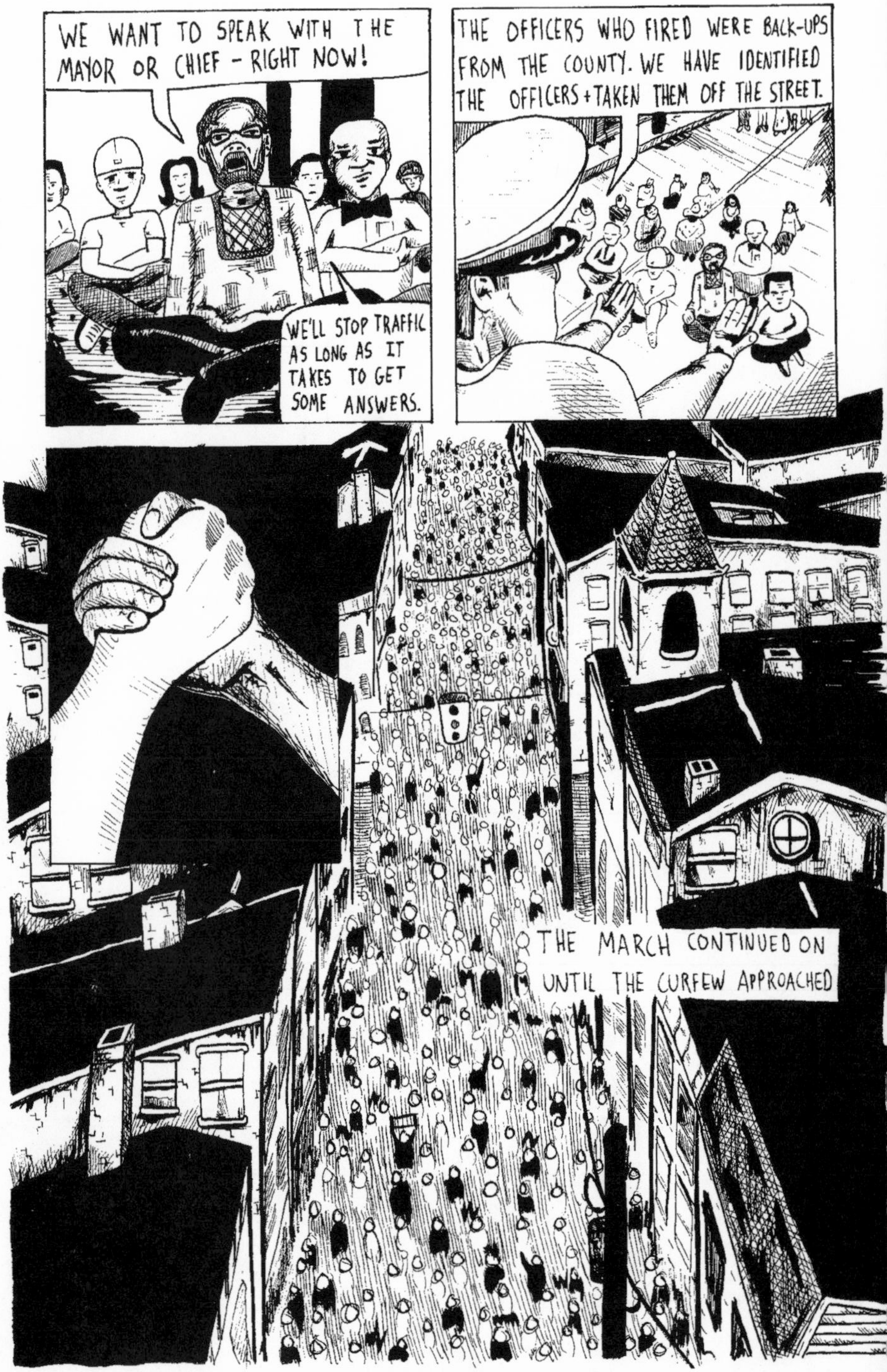
WE WANT TO SPEAK WITH THE MAYOR OR CHIEF - RIGHT NOW!
WE'LL STOP TRAFFIC AS LONG AS IT TAKES TO GET SOME ANSWERS.
THE OFFICERS WHO FIRED WERE BACK-UPS FROM THE COUNTY. WE HAVE IDENTIFIED THE OFFICERS + TAKEN THEM OFF THE STREET.
THE MARCH CONTINUED ON UNTIL THE CURFEW APPROACHED

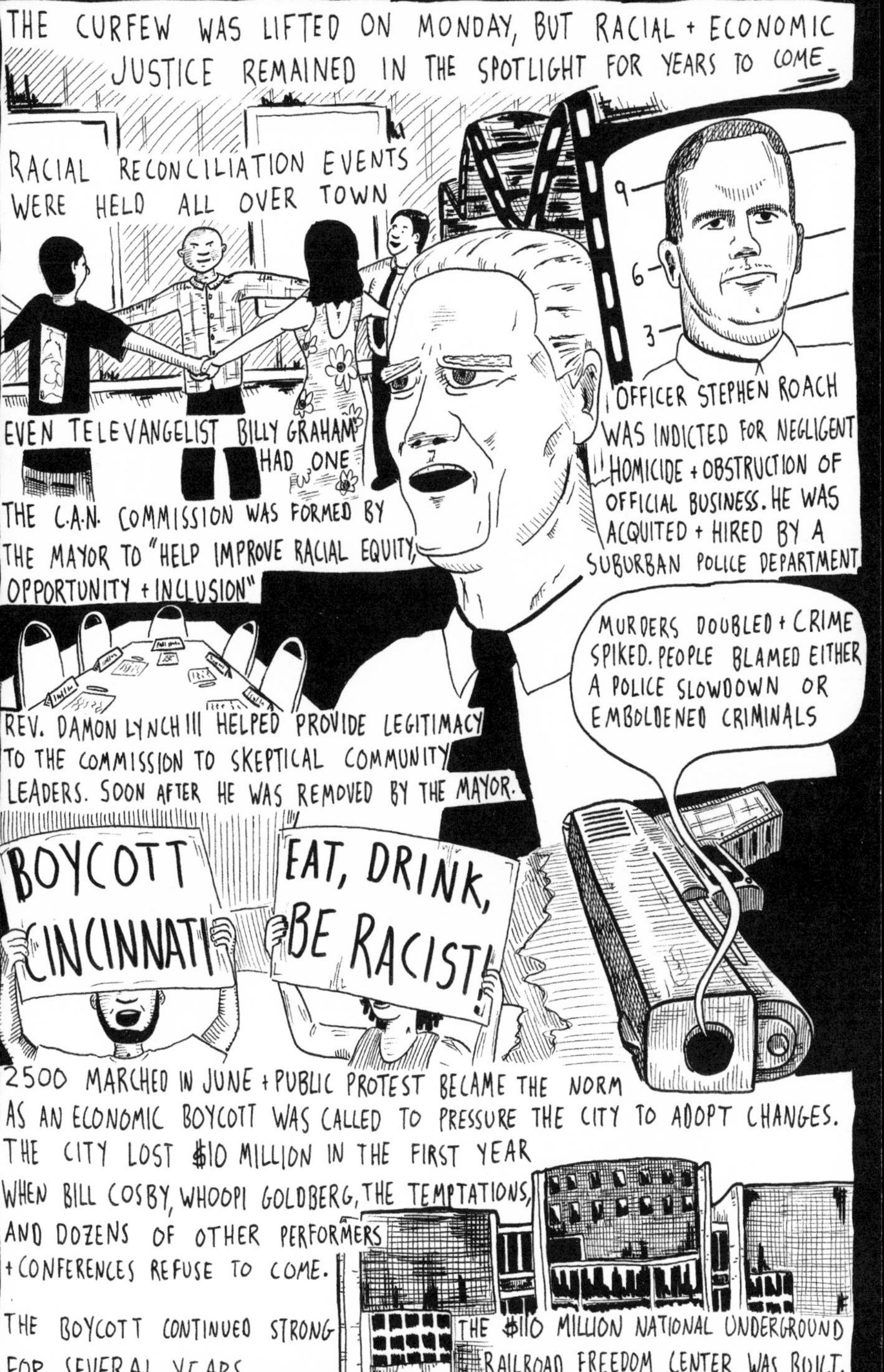
THE CURFEW WAS LIFTED ON MONDAY, BUT RACIAL + ECONOMIC JUSTICE REMAINED IN THE SPOTLIGHT FOR YEARS TO COME.
RACIAL RECONCILIATION EVENTS WERE HELD ALL OVER TOWN
EVEN TELEVANGELIST BILLY GRAHAM HAD ONE
THE C.A.N. COMMISSION WAS FORMED BY THE MAYOR TO "HELP IMPROVE RACIAL EQUITY, OPPORTUNITY + INCLUSION"
9
6
3
OFFICER STEPHEN ROACH WAS INDICTED FOR NEGLIGENT HOMICIDE + OBSTRUCTION OF OFFICIAL BUSINESS. HE WAS ACQUITED + HIRED BY A SUBURBAN POLICE DEPARTMENT
REV. DAMON LYNCH III HELPED PROVIDE LEGITIMACY TO THE COMMISSION TO SKEPTICAL COMMUNITY LEADERS. SOON AFTER HE WAS REMOVED BY THE MAYOR.
MURDERS DOUBLED + CRIME SPIKED. PEOPLE BLAMED EITHER A POLICE SLOWDOWN OR EMBOLDENED CRIMINALS
BOYCOTT CINCINNATI
EAT, DRINK, BE RACIST!
2500 MARCHED IN JUNE + PUBLIC PROTEST BECAME THE NORM AS AN ECONOMIC BOYCOTT WAS CALLED TO PRESSURE THE CITY TO ADOPT CHANGES.
THE CITY LOST $10 MILLION IN THE FIRST YEAR WHEN BILL COSBY, WHOOPI GOLDBERG, THE TEMPTATIONS, AND DOZENS OF OTHER PERFORMERS + CONFERENCES REFUSE TO COME.
THE BOYCOTT CONTINUED STRONG FOR SEVERAL YEARS.
THE $110 MILLION NATIONAL UNDERGROUND RAILROAD FREEDOM CENTER WAS BUILT.

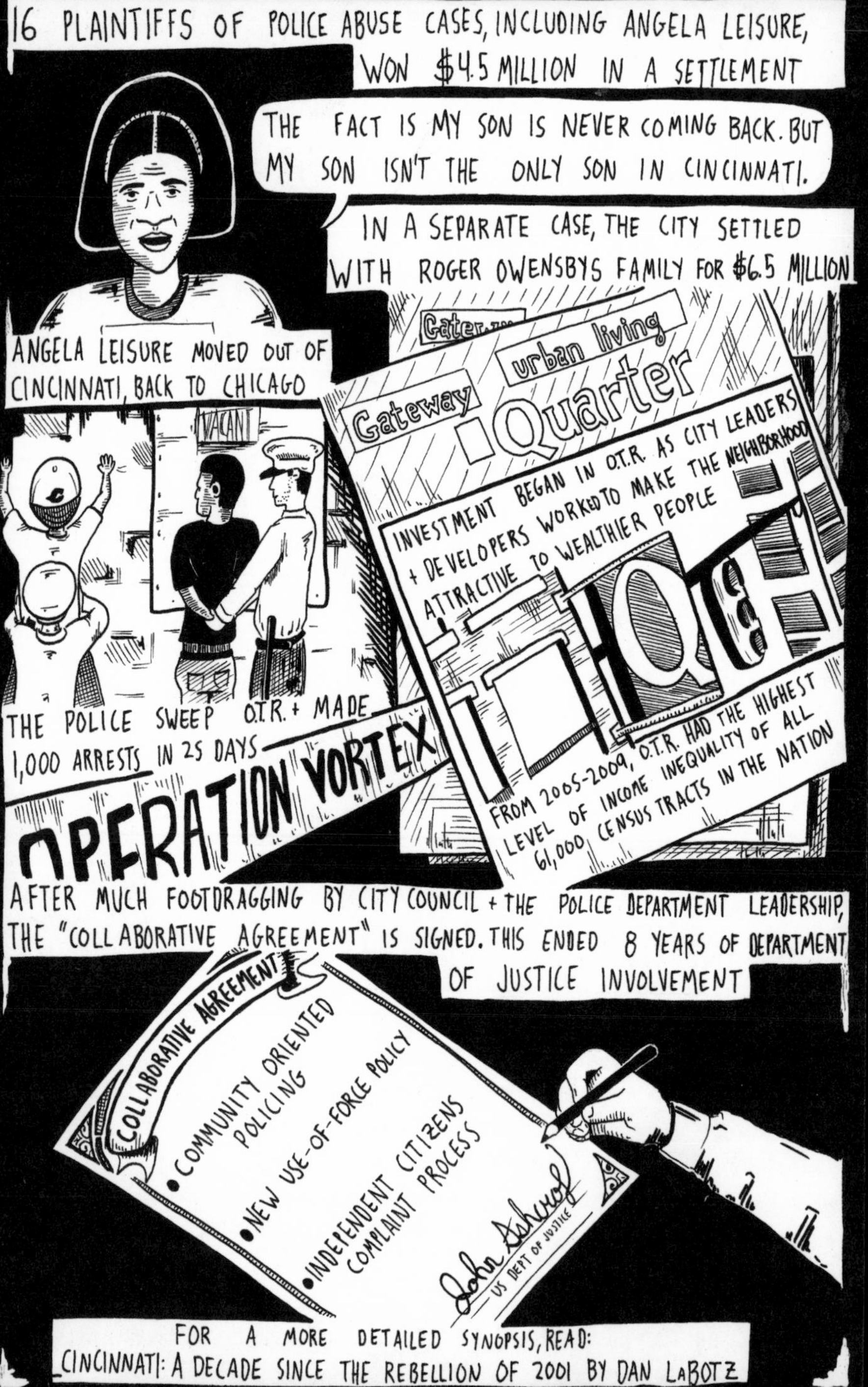
16 PLAINTIFFS OF POLICE ABUSE CASES, INCLUDING ANGELA LEISURE, WON $4.5 MILLION IN A SETTLEMENT
THE FACT IS MY SON IS NEVER COMING BACK. BUT MY SON ISN'T THE ONLY SON IN CINCINNATI.
IN A SEPARATE CASE, THE CITY SETTLED WITH ROGER OWENSBYS FAMILY FOR $6.5 MILLION
ANGELA LEISURE MOVED OUT OF CINCINNATI, BACK TO CHICAGO
VACANT
THE POLICE SWEEP O.T.R. + MADE 1,000 ARRESTS IN 25 DAYS
OPERATION VORTEX
Gateway urban living Quarter
INVESTMENT BEGAN IN O.T.R. AS CITY LEADERS + DEVELOPERS WORKED TO MAKE THE NEIGHBORHOOD ATTRACTIVE TO WEALTHIER PEOPLE
FROM 2005-2009, O.T.R. HAD THE HIGHEST LEVEL OF INCOME INEQUALITY OF ALL 61,000 CENSUS TRACTS IN THE NATION
AFTER MUCH FOOTDRAGGING BY CITY COUNCIL + THE POLICE DEPARTMENT LEADERSHIP, THE "COLLABORATIVE AGREEMENT" IS SIGNED. THIS ENDED 8 YEARS OF DEPARTMENT OF JUSTICE INVOLVEMENT
COLLABORATIVE AGREEMENT
• COMMUNITY ORIENTED POLICING
• NEW USE-OF-FORCE POLICY
• INDEPENDENT CITIZENS COMPLAINT PROCESS
John Ashcroft
US DEPT OF JUSTICE
FOR A MORE DETAILED SYNOPSIS, READ:
CINCINNATI: A DECADE SINCE THE REBELLION OF 2001 BY DAN LABOTZ

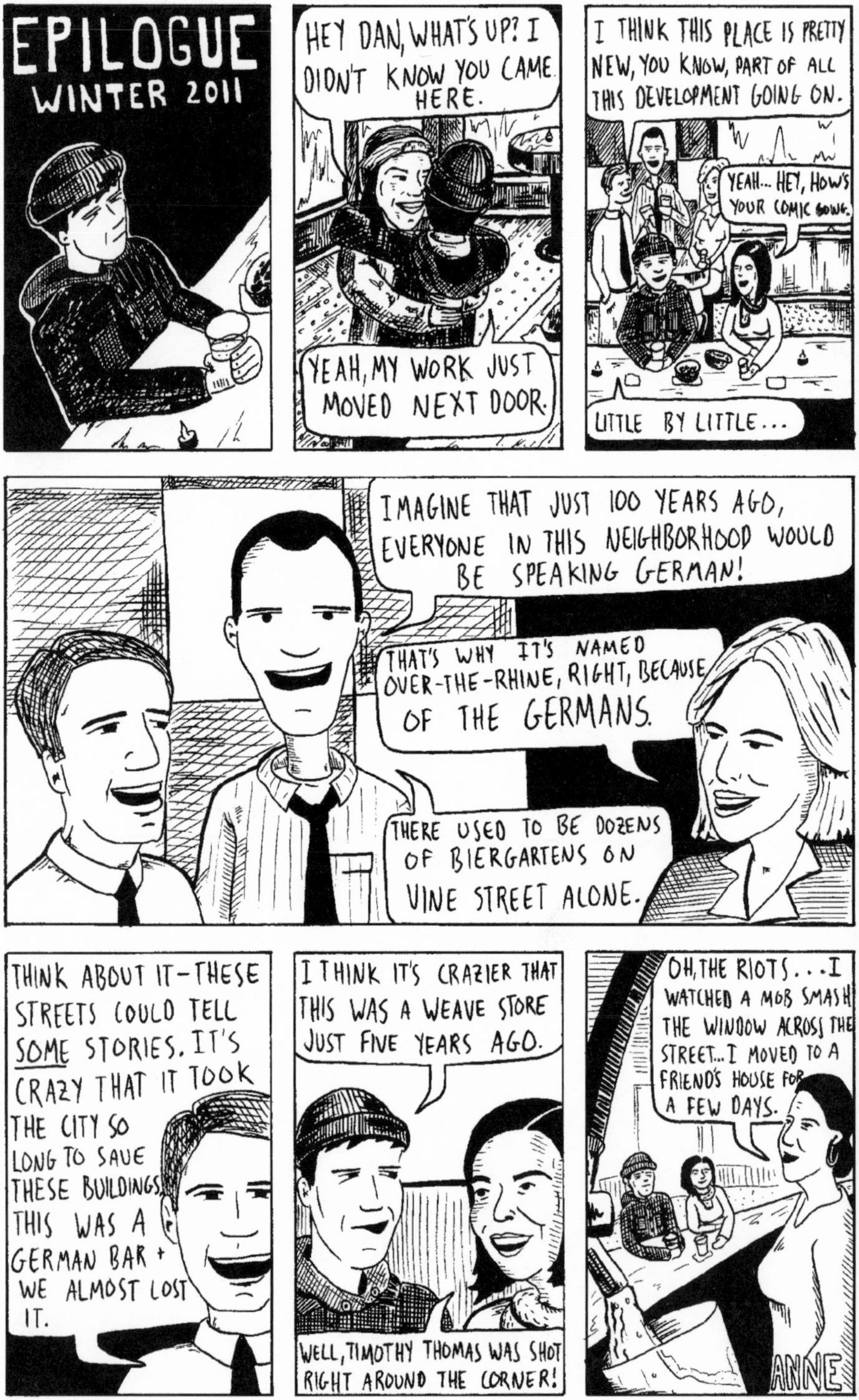
EPILOGUE
WINTER 2011
HEY DAN, WHAT'S UP? I DIDN'T KNOW YOU CAME HERE.
YEAH, MY WORK JUST MOVED NEXT DOOR.
I THINK THIS PLACE IS PRETTY NEW, YOU KNOW, PART OF ALL THIS DEVELOPMENT GOING ON.
YEAH... HEY, HOW'S YOUR COMIC GOING.
LITTLE BY LITTLE...
IMAGINE THAT JUST 100 YEARS AGO, EVERYONE IN THIS NEIGHBORHOOD WOULD BE SPEAKING GERMAN!
THAT'S WHY IT'S NAMED OVER-THE-RHINE, RIGHT, BECAUSE OF THE GERMANS.
THERE USED TO BE DOZENS OF BIERGARTENS ON VINE STREET ALONE.
THINK ABOUT IT—THESE STREETS COULD TELL SOME STORIES. IT'S CRAZY THAT IT TOOK THE CITY SO LONG TO SAVE THESE BUILDINGS. THIS WAS A GERMAN BAR + WE ALMOST LOST IT.
I THINK IT'S CRAZIER THAT THIS WAS A WEAVE STORE JUST FIVE YEARS AGO.
WELL, TIMOTHY THOMAS WAS SHOT RIGHT AROUND THE CORNER!
OH, THE RIOTS...I WATCHED A MOB SMASH THE WINDOW ACROSS THE STREET...I MOVED TO A FRIEND'S HOUSE FOR A FEW DAYS.
ANNE

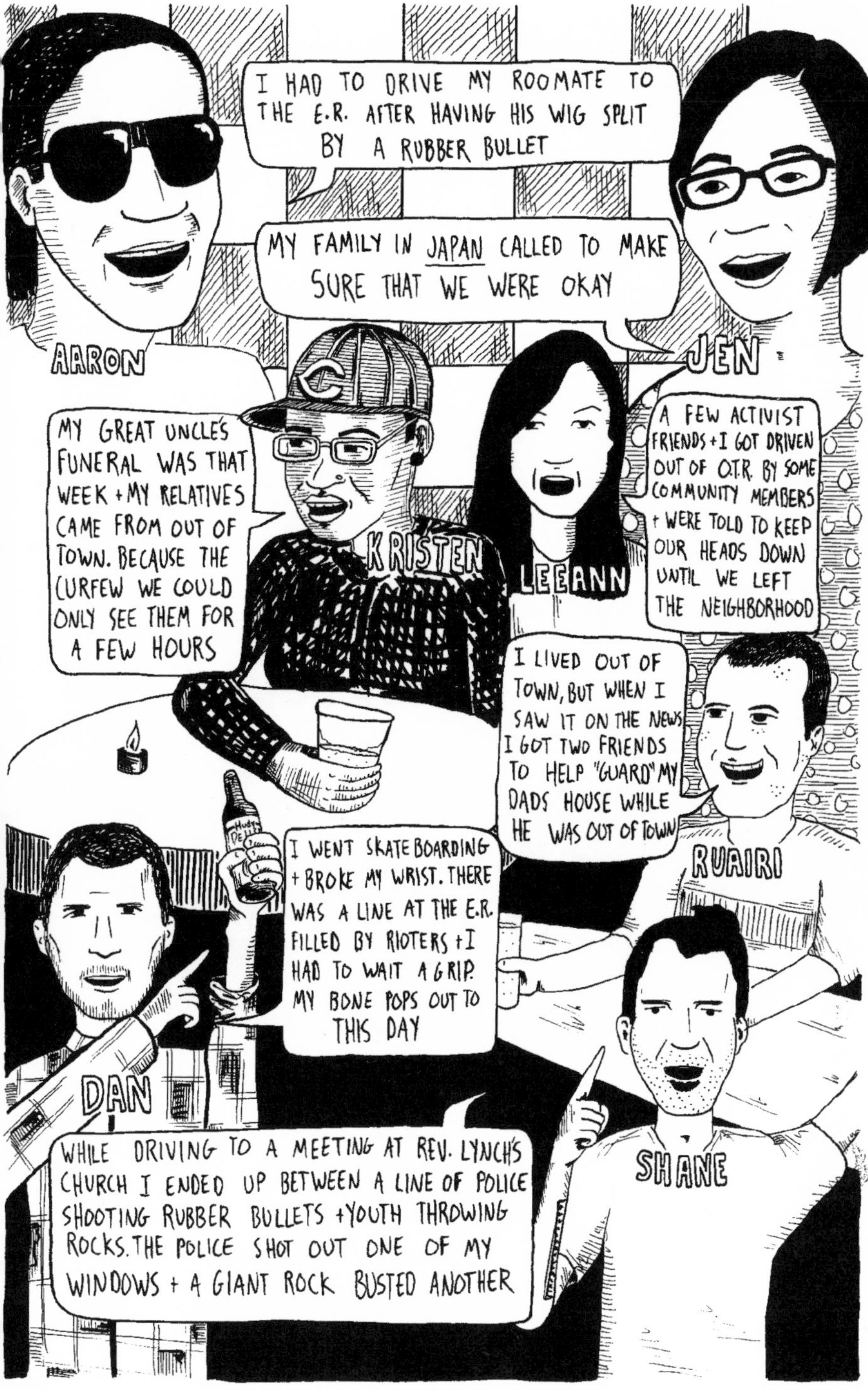
I HAD TO DRIVE MY ROOMATE TO THE E.R. AFTER HAVING HIS WIG SPLIT BY A RUBBER BULLET
MY FAMILY IN JAPAN CALLED TO MAKE SURE THAT WE WERE OKAY
AARON
JEN
MY GREAT UNCLE'S FUNERAL WAS THAT WEEK + MY RELATIVES CAME FROM OUT OF TOWN. BECAUSE THE CURFEW WE COULD ONLY SEE THEM FOR A FEW HOURS
KRISTEN
LEEANN
A FEW ACTIVIST FRIENDS + I GOT DRIVEN OUT OF O.T.R. BY SOME COMMUNITY MEMBERS + WERE TOLD TO KEEP OUR HEADS DOWN UNTIL WE LEFT THE NEIGHBORHOOD
I LIVED OUT OF TOWN, BUT WHEN I SAW IT ON THE NEWS I GOT TWO FRIENDS TO HELP "GUARD" MY DADS HOUSE WHILE HE WAS OUT OF TOWN
RUAIRI
I WENT SKATEBOARDING + BROKE MY WRIST. THERE WAS A LINE AT THE E.R. FILLED BY RIOTERS + I HAD TO WAIT A GRIP. MY BONE POPS OUT TO THIS DAY
DAN
SHANE
WHILE DRIVING TO A MEETING AT REV. LYNCH'S CHURCH I ENDED UP BETWEEN A LINE OF POLICE SHOOTING RUBBER BULLETS + YOUTH THROWING ROCKS. THE POLICE SHOT OUT ONE OF MY WINDOWS + A GIANT ROCK BUSTED ANOTHER

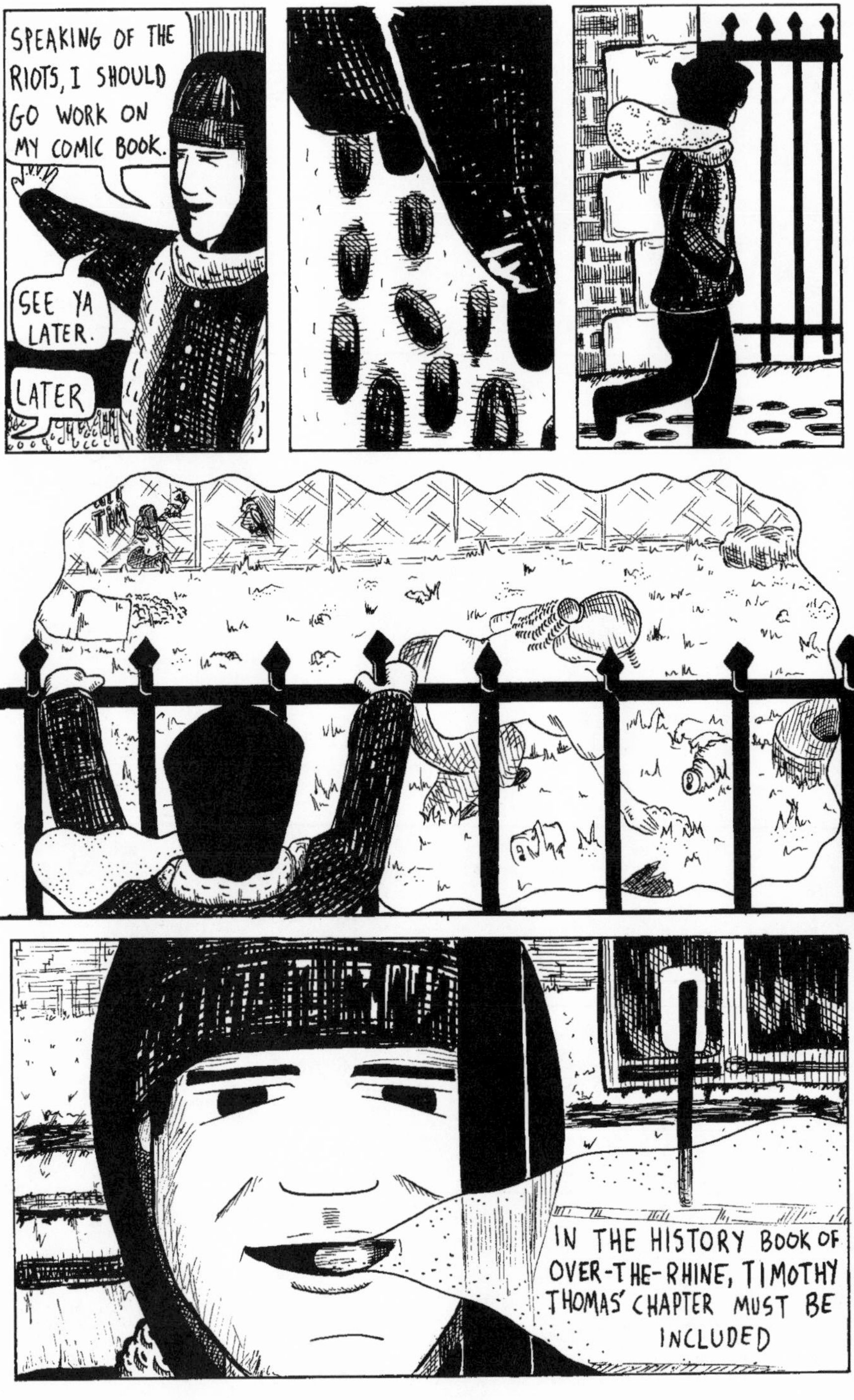
SPEAKING OF THE RIOTS, I SHOULD GO WORK ON MY COMIC BOOK.
SEE YA LATER.
LATER
IN THE HISTORY BOOK OF OVER-THE-RHINE, TIMOTHY THOMAS' CHAPTER MUST BE INCLUDED

BE OUR "BEST FRIEND FOREVER"

Do you love what Microcosm publishes?
Do you want us to publish more great stuff?
Would you like to receive each new title as
it's published?
If you answer "*yes!*" then you should subscribe
to our BFF program. BFF subscribers help
pay for printing new books, zines, and more.
They also ensure that we can continue to
print great material each month! Every time
we publish something new we'll send it to
your door!
Subscriptions are based on a sliding scale
of $10-30 per month. Please give what you
can afford so that we can be sure to send
out more stuff each month. Include your
t-shirt size and month/date of birthday for
a possible surprise!

microcosmpublishing.com/bff

Minimum subscription period is 6 months. Subscription begins the month after
it is purchased. To receive more than 6 months, add multiple orders to your
quantity.

Microcosm Publishing
636 SE 11th Ave. Portland, OR 97214
www.microcosmpublishing.com